# A
# Salad
# Only the
# Devil
# Would
# Eat

# A
# Salad
# Only the
# Devil
# Would
# Eat

## The Joys of
## Ugly Nature

# Charles Hood

Heyday, Berkeley, California

Library of Congress Cataloging-in-Publication Data

Names: Hood, Charles, 1959- author.
Title: A salad only the devil would eat : the joys of ugly nature / Charles
    Hood.
Description: Berkeley, California : Heyday, [2021]
Identifiers: LCCN 2021013502 (print) | LCCN 2021013503 (ebook) | ISBN
    9781597145459 (paperback) | ISBN 9781597145466 (epub)
Subjects: LCSH: Nature--Miscellanea. | Nature--Humor.
Classification: LCC QH81 .H728 2021 (print) | LCC QH81 (ebook) | DDC
    508--dc23
LC record available at https://lccn.loc.gov/2021013502
LC ebook record available at https://lccn.loc.gov/2021013503

Cover Art: Craig Cutler / www.craigcutler.com
Cover Design: Ashley Ingram
Interior Design/Typesetting: Ashley Ingram

All photographs by the author, except bobcat (106), John Haubrich, and author photo (218), Amber Hood.

Published by Heyday
P.O. Box 9145, Berkeley, California 94709
(510) 549-3564
heydaybooks.com

Printed in East Peoria, Illinois, by Versa Press, Inc.

10 9 8 7 6 5 4 3 2 1

FSC
www.fsc.org
MIX
Paper from
responsible sources
FSC® C005010

For Abbey, the still point of the turning world.

# Contents

# I
# Heart
# Ugly
# Nature

Once upon a time I lived at the beach, and not just any beach, but one of the good ones, Newport Beach in Orange County. A hashtag search delivers 2.3 million Instagram hits; if you stand at the end of Newport's wood-planked pier on winter mornings, Catalina Island looks close enough to touch. I was not there the day a masked booby showed up, but I have seen a sea turtle, a bloom of moon jellies, and a stout man paddling a paddleboard completely naked. Coffee in hand, sitting on the front steps of my rental cottage, I would admire the early surfers jogging past in neon-trimmed neoprene, shortboards clamped under blond arms. I envied their urgency and zeal. According to their wet suits, their names were O'Neill and Rip Curl. Their girlfriends were even prettier and more fit than they were. I had a surfboard too, but it didn't do me much good. Any wave obvious enough and slow enough for me to catch just petered out in the kelpy slop thirty seconds later. Mostly, I used it to prop open the door when I brought in the groceries.

Newport was beautiful, but life there was complicated since I was married yet separated and we had a baby on the way and no real plan. We also only had access to the rental house for nine months out of the year; in summers we had to move out, putting everything in storage and living out of our truck. With the baby and all, a tenure-track job seemed like a good way to start over. Rumor had it a college in the Antelope Valley would be hiring two, maybe three English teachers. This is the Joshua tree highlands part of the desert, north of the Inland Empire, east of Los Angeles, south of the High Sierra. The tall, vigorous mountains of Angeles Crest separate the Antelope Valley from the rest of Southern California. It is (and probably always has been) a bit lost in time, like a down-market Shangri-La. My hope was to be invited for a campus visit, and if so, before the interview I could bird the nearby town of Mojave (checking for spring migrants), and afterwards, if I got out in time, take a quick cruise through the Lancaster Sewage Ponds.

Water in the desert is a rare thing, and rare places attract rare birds. Among the most legendary of these, a shorebird called a Polynesian tattler had been discovered at the sewage ponds one July day by Jon Dunn. I don't know what Dunn said out loud in that moment, but if it had been me, I would have said *holy shit.*

The Polynesian tattler breeds in Siberia and winters in the South Pacific, and Dunn's how-lucky-can-you-get sighting was the first record south of the Aleutians. Would there ever be another one? The only way to know: keep looking.

My job application made the cut and I was told to show up on a Friday in May. I drove out the night before and stayed at Motel 6. The day started great, with perfect temperature and no wind, the trees dripping with birds. I logged eleven species of warbler by midday, including two rare ones for California—a black-and-white warbler and a northern waterthrush. I drove Highway 14 back to Lancaster, had lunch, then changed into my suit in the restaurant parking lot. I took out my earrings and put on my wedding ring. I pushed my fingers through my hair. *Show time.*

The committee was cordial but skeptical: I had a quirky CV that included everything from ESL to photography to a Fulbright in ethnopoetics. There was some tech writing, volunteer work in a marsh, a letter of reference from a poet laureate. It didn't add up. They needed somebody to commit to a lifetime of teaching remedial English. The Academic VP wanted to know, had I taken the wrong exit? Did I even know where I was?

I understood why she had to ask. It has a bad rap, the Antelope Valley. The Antelope Valley is the place where old sofas crawl to the ends of dirt roads to die. Fame touches the Antelope Valley rarely, though Tom Selleck was part owner of a shopping plaza and came out to cut the ribbon. In the 1920s, Judy Garland's family had a house here; it later became a homeless shelter and then was gutted by fire. Frank Zappa grew up here and that should count for something, but once he got out, he refused to come back, not even when offered a pile of money to give a single speech. In Senegal I was once asked if the antelope in my valley were good to eat. Yes, and in fact so good that we ate them all. Even the Pacific Crest Trail goes around the valley instead of crossing it, sticking to the high ground like a matron avoiding a load of spilled manure.

I took a risk and told the committee the truth, that my next stop was the sewage ponds, and talked about birds and deserts and how that afternoon's target species, Franklin's gull, was named after Sir John Franklin, a polar explorer who died of scurvy in 1847. According to campus legend, I ended by standing on the table, flapping my elbows and imitating bird calls.

Soon enough the job came, and so did the baby; the marriage came back together and then went away again and finally stayed gone for good. Years passed. I learned that xeric landscapes suited me. Not just the Mojave where I have lived thirty-odd years, but all the others—Black Rock Desert in Nevada and Atacama in Chile, the Gobi and the Namib, the Kalahari and the Taklamakan. "The desert is where God is and man is not," or so explains Victor Hugo. Challenge accepted.

Rather than hosting the nomads of Burning Man or the architecture of John Lautner, my desert is more about cars that don't run—all my neighbors own at least one—and mailboxes wallpapered with lost dog announcements. That's why this is the very best place to be a nature writer. The birds are here at the sewage ponds (and the sod farms, in the case of wintering mountain plovers), while back in Newport Beach, people are still trying to find a place to park. I have always been attracted to the idea of making art from trash, perhaps because I was raised by the generation carved from the stob wood of the Great Depression. They slid directly from that experience into the communal frugality of the Second World War. In that way of being and making, an empty Maxwell House coffee can might be reincarnated as a flower vase or a sorting bin for bent nails, or as the chalice into which one pours bacon grease, to be stored on the back shelf of the fridge. You can use bacon lard to grease a skillet or top off a bird feeder. A world in which I wait for perfect light in a perfect meadow before taking a picture of the perfect bird is going to be a world where I can only "do" nature for ten minutes once every twenty years. But when I embrace the cactus wren singing from a hillside that includes dirt bike scars and ragged mounds of old carpet, I can have all the birds and nature I want, every day of the year.

Even my dog Lucy was a rescue from the pound, and bless her, but she's a bit of a muddle. She is afraid of sneezes and all aspects of carrots, and as a corgi-shepherd-lemur mix, her legs are too short while her butt is too long. Due to various dental mishaps, she has fewer teeth than the average cast member in *Tiger King*. She can't decide if she wants to play with pigeons or eat them, and any puddle, no matter how fetid, clearly exists only to be waded into and sampled deeply. If there is a passing siren, one must stop and howl—I am expected to join in as well—and anything peed on during the outbound half of a journey has to be marked again twice as vigorously on the return leg, just to be sure the territorial claims have not gone stale in the intervening hour. She would prefer some assistance from me in this, but Lucy understands solidarity has its limits.

Spring of 2020 hit us all like the comet that killed the dinosaurs. You know it's going to be bad when even the biker bars have to close. Some of my classes switched to Zoom, while other gigs circled the drain a few times and *shlurped* away forever. Worse, the shutdown meant no more birding trips. My wife, Abbey, and I ended up sharing a house but not a schedule. We got along fine, but she had to work the hours I was free, and same for me the other way around. If I couldn't travel or even work in my campus office, at least I could take long walks. By necessity, Lucy and I became topographic locavores.

I live in Palmdale, which as my kids liked to point out, has few palms and no dales. (They also called it "Yawn-dale.") A roadcut here is popular as a cover shot for geology textbooks because the sheer face reveals layers of stone folded in half by the San Andreas Fault. Overhead, blue sky stretches from the aircraft assembly plants straight up to the edge of outer space; in the promo brochures, the Chamber of Commerce brags about 360 flying days a year. Parts of Palmdale look bougie, even upscale, and on the good side of town there is a Trader Joe's and a Barnes and Noble. On the bad side of town (which of course is where I live), development has been more casual, even haphazard, and tracts of modest, mostly blue-collar homes alternate with vacant lots and sections of creosote edgeland that collectively are not quite original desert, not quite exurban wasteland, but an in-between zone of once-grazed, sometimes-trash-filled, always fascinating possibility.

If society shuts down, the desert is a good place to ride it out. From my front door, it only takes me a few minutes to reach open terrain. Lucy and I traverse two blocks of the same one- and two-story houses, most with a single, scruffy yard tree: Bradford pear, London plane, Italian cypress, Biltmore ash. Some of the trees have white flowers in spring, some have yellow foliage in fall, but all require an obscene amount of water. Slowly my neighborhood is converting to xeriscape, and I now have a palo verde tree and a desert catalpa in the front yard—instead of the sidewalk-lifting, water-pipe-breaking, beetle-infested ash tree that once was—along with agaves and sages and wildlife-appropriate groundcover. Other houses have drip-line-fed fruit trees or zig-zagged paving stones or the Zen calm of homemade rock gardens. Small changes can make swift differences: once we put in the new plants, we had butterflies and hummingbirds visiting the very first day.

At the end of the block, Lucy and I have to decide, left or right? There are no formal parks or nature preserves nearby, but we can connect the open sections into a route that could last all day if we wanted. On most rambles we limit ourselves to out-and-backs of a few miles. The goal is not raw mileage but to learn the land by walking and thinking, looking and touching, writing and noticing. Or at least, those are my goals; Lucy's are more territorial. If her ambitions could be summed up by a single artwork, it would be *Westward the Course of Empire Takes Its Way*.

As our walks take us to new places, I name previously unnoticed features: Railroad Ditch, Church Ditch, Nadaland, Salt Cedar Fields 1 and 2, Field of Broken Bikes. For most people this landscape looks like it has been hit about ten times with the ugly stick and left for dead. The bushes are spare and prickly, Joshua trees can't decide if they are small trees or large toilet brushes, and everywhere, everywhere, the yellow static of cheatgrass fills up all the spare pieces of dirt, leaving no room for slower, more indigenous grasses, and always ready to catch fire at the first flickering touch of a car-tossed cigarette.

Yet I *like* this desert. I feel at home here. On paper, this does not seem inevitable. In fact, on paper, my local plant list sounds like a salad only the devil would eat: bitterbrush, burro weed, creosote, jumping cholla, Mormon tea. If we take away labels, the plants themselves must be praised for their tenacity and admired for their small, miraculous, life-affirming flowers. At work I suppose I have the same ability to stay on task as anybody else— the bar is not set very high, in any case—but once outside, each new color or detail distracts me. It's mid-March and mornings are still chilly, but is that cluster of chrome yellow the glow of early daisies? Let me lift this plywood and find out. Yes, Wallace's woolly daisy, *Eriophyllum wallacei*, sage green and hardly bigger than a Ritz cracker. The tiny spoon-shaped leaves would make good toboggins for ladybugs.

Burro weed or burro bush or *Ambrosia dumosa* or white bursage or *hey, are these sticks even alive or what?* fills in the gaps between the taller, more dominant creosote bushes, and like creosote, it spaces itself out evenly, one plant per magic circle. The root systems produce a chemical that tells other roots to clear off, like the collision warning signals on fancy cars. It is two feet tall, and when not in flower, it looks like a midget sagebrush, a rugged little shrub with small leaves that drop off when a drought lasts too long. (Identify a leafless plant by very thin stripes on the stems.) Flowers are yellowy green, and wind pollinated—*achoo,* so much pollen thrown into the air at once, really rough on my allergies—and anybody who has hiked even one hour in the desert has probably walked past it, though almost nobody bothers to learn its name or bend down close enough to notice the Cirque du Soleil of insects that leap and crawl and drill and make babies among its bonsai leaves and seeds.

Beauty—and I am now quoting Roger Scruton—"can be consoling, disturbing, sacred, profane; it can be exhilarating, appealing, inspiring, chilling." But beauty is rarely identified as inherent to sticks, thorns, goatheads, or roadside weeds. We are trained to value large over small, green over brown, lush over sere, smooth over rough, pristine over altered. In movies like *Mad Max,* the post-apocalyptic landscape is always the desert; in *Lawrence of Arabia,* the desert brings out Lawrence's best qualities but also his worst. I think one reason we call an abandoned lot ugly (if we call it anything at all) is that it is not green, not finalized. Tentative things bother us. Make up your mind, dirt: what *are* you? Except if it were green, it would be neither lot nor abandoned; it already would be a park or somebody's house or a Weyerhaeuser tree farm or halfway through escrow or stuck in court or in some way already assimilated into the expected productivity of modern life. Search for "nature images" and you'll end up with horizontal-format, middle-distance photographs filled with a saccharine abundance of trees, meadows, clouds, and water features (usually lakes or waterfalls). A subcomponent of the genre includes one or two hikers, often young, sometimes female, usually Anglo. In page after page of outdoor equipment catalogs or search results, not much bitterbrush or ceanothus or native blackberry on offer. Not much variety. Not much reality. It's like looking at a children's primer from the 1950s, where the caption would say "The happy family goes on vacation." The happy white dad would be driving, the happy air would be blue and crystalline, and in the backseat the happy white kids would be so ruddy cheeked and giddy it was like they had been topped off with helium.

That is not any family I've ever lived in, even the happy ones. It is also not like any nature I have hiked in. Real woods are messy, complex, full of contrradictions and compromises. I prefer terms like "blended nature," which is to say, nature that is native *and* nonnative, blood related *and* adopted, attractive *and* past its sell-by date. I have come to prefer ugly nature best: at least it's not going anywhere. Nobody can take it away from me, nobody can ruin it or lock it up or break my heart by just not caring. If my desert were more Edenic, it would have been built out long ago. Another good thing? Open land, unallocated to any goal and exempt from any purpose, allows for open play. In the Field of Broken Bikes I once saw a gopher snake and a coyote, but some of the most interesting topography is formed by kids riding bikes and digging forts, creating a series of hard-packed dips and launchpads. If I am on my mountain bike, then Lucy and I pelt along in a side-by-side race: who can hit the highest mound first, trying to grab big-time air?

If my wife, Abbey, were present in this essay, she might now say, *Tell these nice people how many times you have broken your wrists. Show them the bent bike rims, the scars on your knee. Tell them about your toes that even with surgery never healed straight.* Luckily, she is not here, and aside from me saying, "Kids, always wear your helmet," we can carry on enjoying how nicely the sunlight glints off broken glass and continue listening for the warning whistles of the squirrels. These are California or Beechey ground squirrels, dun gray with grizzled shoulders and light speckles down the back, and they are Lucy's very special frenemies. The lookout watches from a pyramid of broken concrete, chirping updates and directing the others how to dash back and forth in front of her—the left squirrel goes right, the right squirrel goes left, each one zipping down a hole with minutes to spare, laughing as the dog trips, poor thing—short legs, but very eager. Lucy loves it (and falls for their feints and dodges every time).

To reach that site we have to zig left on a street named East Avenue S-8 and then zag right on Forty-Fifth East. That road becomes dirt and doesn't really go anywhere, but its name reminds us we can never fully escape the grid. The founding fathers were so literal, so bankrupt of imagination, they named the streets not after presidents or zoo animals or circus acts (or the landforms and history of the place itself), but for the sequential letters of the alphabet. Avenue A starts at the Kern County line, and each one-mile increment counts out a new letter. Numbered crossroads keep pace: Forty-Fifth East is exactly half a mile from Fortieth, which is one perfectly measured mile from Thirtieth East. We could have had poetry and Picasso and instead we were handed a xerox of graph paper. Where the hills rise up, where the fault lines run, where we might want to follow an arroyo's meanders and shady places, those features do not matter: the grid rules everything, subduing all lesser cartographies. Some people find structure reassuring. I am inclined to agree with Robert Venturi, the architect famous for a book called *Learning from Las Vegas*. To Venturi, "Disharmony has tension, poignancy, quality, and beauty."

Just before the bike field, some accident of grading has left one ditch by the railroad tracks lower than the other, and the low parts stay wet with runoff and groundwater most months of the year. Arroyo willows cluster in thickets dense as a British hedgerow, and behind that green wall is where the coyotes live, or so I suspect. We can hear them at night, even see them midday, and along the muddy edges of Railroad Ditch I can find their quick trotting tracks, but their actual den site remains a mystery to me.

Bobcats are possible, but I don't expect them often in this corner of Palmdale. Once about every other year a fire-addled mountain lion gets treed in somebody's yard and has to be darted and carried back to the piney woods. Gray foxes are a mix of cinnamon and slate blue, and judging by roadkill and postings in iNaturalist, they are in the foothills nearby but don't reach my township. What I've been really hoping to see is the big-eared, big-eyed kit fox. Kit foxes are slim, tan desert foxes—smallest wild dogs in North America—and one population, the San Joaquin kit fox, has been on the endangered list since 1967. To the surprise of all, San Joaquin kit foxes have begun to move into urban Bakersfield, a Central Valley city that's culturally and ecologically similar to the Antelope Valley. By 2019, surveys estimated Bakersfield had a population of four hundred or even five hundred foxes.

Turns out, these animals appreciate the same vacant lots I do. Researchers of road improvement efforts in Bakersfield discovered that "kit foxes commonly use undeveloped lands (vacant lots, fallow crop fields), storm water catchment basins (sumps), industrial areas (manufacturing facilities, shipping yards), commercial areas (office and retail facilities), manicured open space (parks, schools, golf courses), and linear rights-of-way (canals, railroads, power line corridors)." On the campus of Cal State Bakersfield, I came out of a meeting at dusk one day and watched a kit fox work its way through the parking lot, peeing on the tires of each chrome-hubbed, lifted, four-wheel-drive truck. One claim for macho status was being met and overlaid by another, more liquid claim. (Lucy says she entirely approves.)

In England, a phrase for brownfields and forgotten bits is "accidental countryside." Of course, in England they also say that a car has four tyres and one parks a car at the kerb, so we can't always trust the Brits for good linguistic leadership. But this idea does have merit. In learning the neighborhood by foot, Lucy and I are surprised how quickly we can go from houses to non-houses and from closed systems to open ones. In a car one connects destinations point by point ("I am driving to the store now"), often overlooking the blank places in between. In actuality, there are no blank places, only unseen-by-us places. And on average, those gaps all have their own botanical hierarchies. In my area, the center of the hierarchy is burro weed's big brother, creosote.

Another word for creosote is greasewood. Each spindly bush is six feet tall, six feet around, and spaced out six feet from the next one. The branches spike up from a central point on the ground but in a rather parsimonious bouquet, since the waxy leaves are barely half an inch long. A central taproot supports an alliance of surface-level rootlets fanned out in a huge radius; when it comes to water, creosote does not take even the feeblest drizzle for granted. When I went to college, I was told that each bush leaks poison to sterilize the soil and hence keep other plants at bay. Probably not true but it I want it be, so I repeat it here, reminding you that it's unreliable nonsense from a cranky old man. What I don't approve of is the one-name-for-two things problem, since the black ooze painted on railroad ties is also called creosote. That product comes from coal tar, not plants—the plant is named for the preservative, not the other way around.

Creosote has shown me to be a failure as an herbalist. Gary Nabhan and others document indigenous uses ranging from mending arrow shafts to treating tuberculosis. Inspired by its many medicinal properties, I once tried cooking sprigs of creosote into a healing broth. Wrong trousers, Gromit: all I managed to do was stink up the kitchen and coat the bottom of our best sauce pan with a patina of black goo that even steel wool couldn't scrub clean.

No territory has ever named creosote's small yellow blossoms as state flower, yet taken as a whole, creosote outnumbers the poppy a trillion to one. Botanist Matt Ritter calls creosote "the toughest desert plant." It is the first thing listed on the National Park Service site for plants of Death Valley and the last thing I smell at night, on warm days of spring rain. This special odor comes from defensive measures. As the Mojave Project explains, "The combination of oils and waxes (with additional phytochemicals and compounds that make up 10 to 20 percent of its dry weight) protects the plant by deflecting ultraviolet radiation and heat exposure, overall transpiration, and water loss."

Lucy reminds me that she is the one who protected those plants from potential invaders like carrots or UFOs, so can she have her treat now? Lucy would chase the jackrabbits through the creosote if she could, but their eyesight is better than hers and they always sprint away first, back legs flying. The last time it snowed we only got a few inches, but I grabbed a trekking pole and camera and went out early; gray, crusty snow documented the crisscrossing tracks of multiple jackrabbits, bush to bush and back again. I had not known we had so many, which reminded me to take more walks after dark. That same morning I also found coyote tracks and the meandering path of something mouse sized, and a splayed pattern of micro-pits that I realized marked where the dawn creosote branches had shed droplets of wet snow.

Writing about it now, it strikes me that this is honest landscape: the world as it is, not how I wish it to be. Nature writing too often drifts into High Church rhetoric. Yet not all forests are pristine; not all ecology heroes are heroic. At the end of his life Ansel Adams drove a Cadillac and John Muir died a de facto millionaire, thanks to his own hard work but thanks also to migrant labor and a well-capitalized inheritance. My hero Ed Abbey threw beer cans out the car window. To leave "nature" islanded in a sea of exalted adjectives is to leave us out of the conversation. Nature is not above us, separate but better. It is us—weeds, warts, and all. When *National Geographic* wanted to do a feature article on tumbleweeds, where did they go to find them? Raise your hand if you were about to say the Antelope Valley. Do you collect hubcaps? Come on down: the bushes are full of them. We can also do tin cans from modern days back to the 1930s.

And yet here's this, too. I never expected to find so many young Joshua trees coming up in roadside fields that were abandoned a generation ago. There is a claim one hears, that Joshua trees only occur two places, the Mojave Desert and the Holy Land. Half right on that. None in the Levant, but the range includes Arizona, California, Nevada, and Utah. Pollinated by moths. Spread through seeds or rhizomes. Named for a fellow in the Bible. The largest Joshua trees might be a few hundred years old, but the smaller ones are just ten or twenty or thirty years old, many coming up out of a creosote's reluctant shade; these young ones look like yuccas and so are easy to overlook.

They are there, the next generation of Joshua trees, and their return is not due to any human intervention—other than neglect. Our best action on behalf of nature may be inaction: stand back and let it do its thing, see what happens. Plants do not need to be beautiful or even picturesque to be ecologically valuable. Some of the Joshua trees in my area wear prayer shawls in the form of shredded plastic bags, this is true. When my friends complain, I tell them I have a ladder and they are welcome to go and tidy things up if they want. True too that many Joshua trees have been burned black and gold by fires, and one Joshua tree I call the Old Gent got knocked crooked by a drunk driver ten, twelve years ago. Yet it grows still, a Leaning Tower of Pisa and fortitude, not giving up.

Hard work being alive, for us as well as the plants. If you've made it this far, give yourself a round of applause. And hard too, looking at the work that still needs to be done. Easy to get discouraged. As I write these words, somewhere there is a dog at the end of a chain, weary and harmed. As I write these words, somewhere a person is hungry, while another person tries to wipe the blood off her face with the hem of her shirt. Yet as I write these words, an oriole is building a nest in the thatched beard of an untrimmed palm tree, and it is letting me watch. As I write these words, a kind of bat called a pipistrelle, small and quick, celebrates sunset and moonrise. As I write these words, water waits in a stream. As I write these words, marsh hawk. As I write these words, mule deer. As I write these words, quartz, obsidian, chert. As I write these words, owl's clover, chicory, lupine, globe gilia, marigold, evening snow.

As I write these words, music and laughter.

As I write these words, hidden nature, ugly nature, abandoned nature, holy nature.

As I write these words, I have been walking a long time, but I am finally arriving, and it feels good to be home.

# The
# Lure
# of the
# List

The birder, the painter, the Devil are always watching, always waiting.

—Toby Ferris, *Short Life in a Strange World*

Billy Idol almost hit me once, gunning a red convertible out of a gas station, scattering pedestrians on the sidewalk. A week later I shared an elevator ride with Rodney Dangerfield, coming up from the parking lot of a now-closed Borders Bookstore in Westwood. Magician Ricky Jay, lobby of the Egyptian Theatre. Keanu Reeves, coming out of a rainy, midnight showing of the director's cut of *Blade Runner*—I think he and I made up 50 percent of the audience. John Cusack, another bookstore. Jim Carey, in his *Man on the Moon* phase, Sunset Boulevard. James Cromwell, the farmer in *Babe*, LACMA. John Milius—he wrote *Dirty Harry* and *Apocalypse Now*, directed *Red Dawn* and *The Wind and the Lion*, created the TV series *Rome*—also Westwood. He was smoking a cigar. Elijah Wood, aka Frodo, in Amoeba Records, Hollywood. And same store, another time, the musician Beck, shopping for vinyl.

Yes, I do keep a movie star list, though I would rather die than ask to take a photo or in any way break the fourth wall. Celebrities? Just be cool and ignore them, other than maybe the slightest nod of recognition—*I see you and agree to abide by the unspoken Code of California Conduct. You do your thing, I do mine. I won't pester you.* Of course, with so many shows and with fewer megastars patrolling the open veldt, it's more often a case of, "Hey, isn't he that guy who was in that thing?" The only time I've seen JLo, she was in Beverly Hills being chased by paparazzi— sad and cruel, like a pack of hyenas trying to hamstring a gazelle. Yet the mythic Hollywood of Musso & Frank did really exist, as I know personally, since my grandfather, a car salesman, was the guy who taught Bette Davis how to drive. Why him? Well, she had just bought a car and somebody had to help her get it off the lot. Might as well be him.

Lists are funny things: life-affirming, joy-giving, usually harmless. Yet listing can slide into being darkly addictive. To be a lister is to be driven by the need to see all of a certain set of things—usually birds, and usually defined by geography. What one counts as legit follows a set of rules, and those rules are provided by regional bodies. So you can have a British list, based off rules adjudicated by the British Ornithologists' Union, or an ABA List (Lower 48, Hawaii and Alaska, all of Canada), watched over by the American Birding Association. In Texas, in the Lower Rio Grande Valley, you can stand on the US side of the river looking into Mexico. The legal division between the two countries is the exact midpoint of the water; you can only count a duck on your ABA list if you're sure it's on your side of the river. Of course, if it veers left and right far enough, the same duck can be counted on two lists at once, ABA and Mexican, plus a Texas state list, and, if you keep one, your year list. In comparison to listers, bird-watchers are casual, not minding if they go to a place and don't chase down and identify every sparrow in every mucky bog. Listers compulsively *do* need to get it all. To miss a thing needed for one's list is—

*oh, it feels so bad my eyes squinch tight and I cannot type.*

In Britain they call hardcore listers "twitchers," not for their nervous facial tics, but in the words of Mark Beaman, "rather the terrible nervousness, the fear of 'dipping out' that we experienced as we drove (often through the night) towards that distant rarity. Would it have gone? Worse, would it leave just before we got there? We 'twitched' with nervousness as we got close to that appointment with destiny." The term even made it onto the telly. In 2001, on *Who Wants to be a Millionaire*, the contestant was asked, "Which of these is a popular term for birdwatcher? (a) Twitcher; (b) Jerker; (c) Blinker; (d) Jumper."

The correct answer of course is only (a), but I would like

to see them all gain steady usage. Most rare birds are storm-blown strays and tend to land on far-off coasts, not close to work, school, family, or mainline trains. Beware the verge, since in Britain—just as can happen here—if a rare bird is reported, too often decorum departs and ethics lapse. According to the *Washington Post*, "Local police were forced to cordon off streets after hundreds of desperate bird-watchers descended on a suburban home in Hampshire when a rare Spanish sparrow fluttered into somebody's garden."

This means certain bird locations can't be made public, for fear of harm. Elf owls are sparrow sized and monkey faced, with round, yellow eyes. World's smallest owl, they can be irritatingly hard to track down—only a dozen pairs breed in California. (They like woodpecker cavities in saguaros; try along the Colorado River.) An elf owl nest was found one spring in Joshua Tree National Park, just three hours from Los Angeles. If the news had gotten out, a hundred people would have arrived by nightfall, playing owl recordings and wandering around with spotlights until the birds dropped dead from exhaustion.

Fearing for both the safety of the owls and the owls' trees, the National Park Service imposed a news embargo. It worked; during breeding season, no whisper of the owl's location leaked out, and the now-empty trees grow in what the CIA would call "an undisclosed location."

Nature lends itself to lists, or at least nature as we practice it now, with an emphasis on nouns and range maps and endangered species. As soon as we put a name to something, that means it can be ranked and counted. Rank gives value, at successive steps of the ziggurat. Value to the lister ("I do not have this yet, therefore I covet it"), value to the environmental managers ("we have too much of this thing but not enough of the other thing"), value to policy makers ("we must enact better protection—if the real estate lobby doesn't object"), and value to media producers and the public they serve, since the last, the first, the largest, the oldest are most newsworthy.

It all starts with names and relative abundance. Birds are good because they are everywhere and have a lot of variety. Counting trees could be a good choice too. They are not going to fly off, and they come in more varieties than many people would guess. California has seventeen native species of pine tree and twenty-odd oaks. Black oak, island oak, scrub oak, Engelmann oak— enough species to make seeing them all a tough job, yet few enough that as a to-do list you could, in theory, tick all the native oaks in one intense, tree-centric year. You might drive a few thousand miles, but you could do it.

If you want to launch a list, consider these four factors:

(1) Size and visual appeal of the target taxa. Mites are too small and ticks too icky, but dragonflies and wildflowers, those

make good choices: you could list those because they are pretty to look at and you can see them easily, often without binoculars.

(2) Discrete boundaries and a known taxonomy. A list has to be something we can ken. At least in North America, lichens are too poorly differentiated and their ranges too imperfectly known for that group to be good listing fodder. We do not have a popular field guide to lichens here in North America; national parks do not give out lichen-spotting trail maps.

(3) Ability to compare one's own ranking against others. If you're the only one looking for freshwater snails in alpine lakes, that really isn't a list, that's just a sad obsession. Yet amateur astronomers surveying the night sky can work their way through the Messier Objects, ticking off M8, the Lagoon Nebula; or M101, the Pinwheel Galaxy. Take up the Messier list and you can join a group of like-minded people who can share in your successes, sympathize with your misses, encourage your do-overs. You also now have a base level from which rank can be established. Best of all, there are only 110 Messier Objects total, so a complete set is doable. Even companies can keep lists. One tour agency based in Britain, Birdquest, has combined its separate trips into one master list that has now reached 10,450 bird species.

(4) It's much easier to have rankings if there is a body or authority that can make the call about what's ethical or unethical. Sometimes it is casual—you just agree to abide by the social

norms of the group—and sometimes more formalized. There is such a thing as the California Bird Records Committee, and they understand that theirs is a sacred trust. Like Gnostics, they are the keepers of the book of knowledge, hidden deep in the cave of records and guarded by the flames of eternal vigilance. The official bird list changes every few months, as new records arrive or shifts in taxonomy require the entire puzzle to be taken apart and put back together in a new, updated order. It is always exact—no guesses or approximations allowed—and always number specific. "Of the 676 species on this official California checklist," their website says, "13 are established introductions, one has been extirpated within historical times, and one is in the process of being reintroduced but is not yet established. An additional five species of uncertain natural occurrence are included in a supplemental list at the end."

All sounds a bit anorak, doesn't it? That's the British term for a geek or nerd—the proverbial trainspotter, obsessively keeping track of engine models and errant liveries. The word also refers to a kind of windbreaker with no zipper that you struggle to pull over your head. We imagine a sodden fellow standing by the tracks in the rain, desperately waiting for something to happen. It is not a sexy hobby. In between Bakersfield and Mojave, American trainspotters make a pilgrimage to the Tehachapi Loop, a site where trains ascend a steep grade via a large-radius circle. If a train is long enough—a bit over a mile total—it crosses above its own caboose, like a snake eating its own tail. Weather here is usually mild: no anoraks needed.

When it comes to birds, not just nouns count. Verbs are countable too: the behaviors one has seen or photographed. Frank Pitelka taught at UC Berkeley for fifty years and commuted between California and sites in Alaska, where he saw some of the rarest birds on the American list. Even so, he only added to his own tally in special circumstances. According to Kimball Garrett, ornithology collections manager at the Natural History Museum of Los Angeles County, "Frank always swore that the *only* list he kept was of bird species seen copulating (the birds copulating, that is, not him)."

More people keep bird lists than generally gets recognized. On May 9, 2020, there was a global "big day," when spotters around the world all logged records into a website called eBird during one twenty-four-hour day. In that time, 51,135 birders collectively noted 6,507 species of birds, reporting 122,000 checklists from 175 islands, territories, outposts, and countries. This effort contributed to the 20,286,678 combined sightings for the month of May. As a summary review pointed out, "There are now more than 500,000 eBirders who have contributed sightings from out their windows, on the way to work, or during visits to parks, ponds, and fields."

These are some seriously big numbers. In figuring out why people do it, some say that listing helps us organize thoughts and experiences while also validating effort. Because they are accumulative, lists are a way of tracking how seriously we've committed to a given field of study. It's not just that I have a ruff—a stray shorebird from Europe named for the fancy neck plumage of breeding males—ticked on my California state bird list; what really spangles my braids is having seen it in all the Southern California counties. To do so took ten hardcore years, plus moderate skill. Picking one out of a shimmery cluster of nearly identical shorebirds, especially in heat haze or if you're zonkers with fatigue after an all-night drive, earns you the Roger Tory Peterson merit badge several times over. In California, fall migration for shorebirds starts in June and peaks in August and September, lasting into November. To plan a November visit to the Salton Sea falls within the realm of normalcy, but August? When it is 110 degrees and the humidity leaks off the tamarisk in fat, sticky, corrosive drops? Climbing K2 is for wusses. Summer at the Salton Sea is where the seriously fanatical side of outdoor study happens. Take a deep breath and plunge in.

As geographical units go, counties provide a workable radius for listing, given that the state of California as a whole is impossibly huge. I once drove nonstop from Los Angeles to the Oregon border to see a rustic bunting, a drab sparrowy thing that had strayed here from Siberia. It was so many miles, vertically, like going from Italy to Sweden. In contrast, most counties are small enough that you can explore them over a series of weekends. And despite the typically modest size of an average county, if numbers matter (and to some, they really do), impressive totals are still possible. Take Guy McCaskie, who has passed 500 birds on his San Diego County list. Just to be clear, this is not 500 overall in the world, not 500 in the state of California, but 500 just in San Diego and adjacent coastal waters. It is a world record; nobody else has done it, and yet the fact that he *has* done it helps show the rest of us what intensity and dedication can finally achieve.

Seeing live and in person matters. Webcams don't count, and as far as I am concerned, just hearing a bird doesn't either. The reason given is the mockingbird, which extends its vocal options by copying other birds, often with perfect fidelity. You might *want* to count a rare nightbird like Arizona's buff-collared nightjar, something heard more often than seen, but mockingbirds call even in the middle of the night. Until you see the nightjar yourself, you can't be sure that what you heard was that species or a mimic, or even another group of birdwatchers playing a recording the next arroyo over. Medieval pilgrims risked a lot to walk Camino Santiago—the Way of Saint James—in order to receive grace and insight and to worship at shrines made more holy by the presence of relics. Thinking about the Bible in the quiet of your own home village was not good enough: you had to be close enough to the relic to touch it, or at least kneel and pray in very close proximity. Authenticity has a radius, and it's not very large.

With digital cameras and ever-improving lenses, photographs verify sightings but trigger new compulsions; some birders won't count a new bird if they didn't snag a photograph of it. A good photograph is like a head mounted in the trophy hunter's study: "Look, I was there, *and I can prove it.*" Ornithology was originally a shotgun-based science, and as the old saying goes, "What's hit is history and what's missed is mystery." One photograph I wish I had gotten: a Mexican vine snake I saw in a rocky canyon on the Arizona border. It had a black mouth and was hunting lizards, and it draped itself over a bush like a long, wet shoelace. Sorting old slides recently, I decided that I have too many pictures of my twelfth birthday party; I would trade half of those for two or three shots documenting my Glorious Vine Snake Hike in Southeastern Arizona.

Am I a bit nutty to care about which snakes I have and have not seen? I keep a running tally of birds in my head, like it or not, all day, every day. This is not intentional. It just happens, like the way your car's odometer tracks mileage: You do not turn it on or off. It is part of the base mechanism, running whether you want it to or not. I know how many ravens I saw on my way to campus today, just as I can remember how many different species of sea cows, manatees, and dugongs there are in the world. I can tell you the last time I saw western bluebird, and where I was when I saw it. If we drew a Venn diagram with personalities of top listers in one circle and a description of obsessive compulsive personality disorder in another, how much would they overlap? The *Diagnostic and Statistical Manual of Mental Disorders* lists eight symptoms that would indicate if a person has OCPD. The first of these—*the very first one*—says subjects may have OCPD if they are "preoccupied with details, rules, lists, order, organization, or schedules to the extent that the major point of the activity is lost."

But what if listing *is* the point of the activity? Or rather, what if listing is not the point, singular, but one aspect of several parallel and independent pleasures. One can be compelled to do something and yet have ambivalent feelings about it, even hate it. I loved being a hardcore twitcher when I was one, but it feels great to be clean and sober. I miss it but feel relief, just as I am proud of all the places on the map I've been to, yet am guilty over my carbon footprint.

Quitting my bird list was hard. Real life feels so drab in comparison. The usual direction is to keep adding, adding, adding, until poverty or death turn off the meter. But I had to have an intervention with myself and admit that too often I came back from a trip unhappy over something stupid—like not seeing the suchity-such, which Joe Money-Wad had seen only a month earlier. Never mind all the other things I *had* seen. I missed that or this, and it ate at me, thinking how I could have made things better. All listers wrestle with this duality. Jonathan Franzen, novelist first and birder second (but just barely), wrote about this regarding a bird trip to Ghana in his book *The End of the End of the Earth.* Here is Franzen's admission: "It's not that I don't love birds for their own sake. I go birding to experience their beauty and diversity, learn more about their behavior and the ecosystems they belong to, and take long, attentive walks in new places. But I also keep way too many lists. I count not only the bird species I've seen worldwide, but the ones I've seen in every country and every US state I've birded in, and also at various smaller sites, including my backyard, and in every calendar year since 2003. I can rationalize my compulsive counting as an extra little game I play within the context of my passion. But I really am compulsive."

So I am too—past tense and present tense—and I have been to Ghana as well. If Franzen and I happened to meet at a party, in my former life as a lister my first reaction to his mention of the country would have been to ask, with seeming indifference, "Oh, Ghana, yes. Lovely place! So what did you get?" The scorecard has only two columns: "Yes, I saw that bird too," or: "Wait, I missed that one, how did *you* get it?" But by the time Mr. Franzen had visited Ghana, I had been clean for years. And so reading about another's adventures there, I felt no envy, no relapse. In

Ghana, I'd had loads of excellent sightings, and those few things I missed—just easier and healthier not to dwell on them. Did Jonathan Franzen pick up any of my missed species? The better angel of my nature says, "I certainly hope so."

Other organisms besides birds attract their fans and fanatics. The *Lolita* author Vladimir Nabokov tracked butterflies; musician John Cage was a mushroom maven. Just as I managed to ease the throttle on hardcore birding, I got cranked up on new dope: mammal listing. Sweet Jesus, save my soul. Shrews and bats, mustangs and mouse-deer, fossas and fur seals: all types interest me equally. They always have, but suddenly I let myself admit it. It felt good, like being awoken from slumber by the prince's kiss, and each year I plan how many mammal trips I can reasonably afford, and then do 25 percent more than that. As I type this, my newest addition to the list was Alvarez's mastiff bat in the Yucatán, a chocolate brown animal with a thin tail like an eager puppy. It was first named as a species in 2011, and I'm not sure how many people have intentionally seen them, but I assume not many.

As far as elite listers go, in the mammal world I am up there, but I am not tippy-top-highest. My list is okay, but I know perfectly well where I stand in relation to everybody else. Or I *think* I do—I don't publish my totals, and a few others don't either. Usually, though, the big listers' lists are known to all. A year ago

I was with Jon Hall, world's top animal counter, when he got to new mammal number 1,800. Most of us would have trouble naming even 25 kinds—"Lion, tiger, chimp, horse, zebra, and um... lizard? Platypus? Is an octopus a mammal?"—and yet there he is, rounding third and heading for home.

Jon Hall's 1,800th species was found while we were driving in the mountains of Morocco, scanning hillsides with a spotlight. The beast in question was a North African (also called Algerian) hedgehog, and we paused a few minutes to hold up a sign and take photos, then pushed on. True listers do not squander daylight, moonlight, starlight, or torchlight. We had the rest of the night ahead of us and Jon could celebrate later, once he got back to New York. Over the course of a week, other discoveries included hares, jerboas, mice, genets, bats, a newly described species of wolf, a previously unknown site for the North African elephant shrew, and multiple encounters with an absurdly too-cute felid called the sand cat. We only slept four hours a night (sometimes not even two), and one conversation we had was about the probability of landmines on the path we wanted to hike next. Almost everything we came across was new to me, and while I wish Royal Air Maroc had not lost my bags, the trip itself was fabulous.

Sand cats are one of forty wild felids. Nobody has seen them all, but several guys are getting close. With any object of desire, satisfaction comes from completing the set. When I was still working on my bird list, I remember how glad I was to have seen a pine flycatcher in Mexico, because it was my final *Empidonax*—a notoriously look-alike assemblage of small, drab birds. If an empid sings, species ID becomes a bit more possible, but migrants and silent birds in the forest can be real head-scratchers. When I identified the last one, it was a case of double the pleasure, double the fun, since not only was that unit now wrapped up, but it also meant that if I so wished, I never had to struggle over their ID ever again. Any trick that I can use to say *Down, boy, down,* to my ticking obsessions is a good thing. Having seen every one of these pesky flycatchers, whenever the next one flew into view, I could just call it by the larger group name "empid," and not have to worry about which empid it might be.

First, though, you have to get there—you have to complete the set. Let's say you have gone to the hypothetical island of Vino Vino, and three similar birds occur there: the greater hobnob, the lesser hobnob, and the three-striped hobnob. (One thing you can be sure of, all three will have at least three stripes, except the three-striped one, which will have four.) You have long dreamed of seeing these, and you need all three for your list. After you have seen the first two kinds, as the end of the trip draws near, nervousness edges towards panic the closer you get to departure. Where is that bloody three-stripped hobnob? You've looked in all the correct places. *Where is it?* At that point, every hobnob that you find that is not the one you still need just annoys you. Greater hobnob? It was your best friend in the world when you first tried to see one at journey's start. But now they seem to be all over the place—intentionally, willfully *not* being three-striped hobnobs. You want to shoo them away: "Get out of the way you hideous bird, I am trying to see the other one. Stop distracting me!"

Whether you get it or not, listing is never about fibbing. Broadly speaking, chivalry rules, and nobody (or almost nobody) lies about the state of their list. "Stringing" means to bend a sighting so you con yourself into thinking that a probable x (which you don't need) could have been y (which you do). While mistakes happen and our passions can blind us all, nobody wants a stringy list. Welcome to integrity's last stand: a culture in which honesty matters and cheating earns one eternal shame. Information is shared openly and freely, or as freely as the elf owl's safety will allow, and one never claims false sightings, gives spurious directions, blocks another fellow's view, or scares off the animal in question after seeing it first. We may argue over identification, or the origin of a vagrant seagull (natural migrant or ship-assisted pet?), but the basic honor code centers on the values of warrior tribes like those described in *Beowulf*, including honesty, bravery, reliability, and service to the community. As a private guess—and I have no firsthand data on this—I bet more birders would cheat on their marriage vows before they would lie about their life lists.

I once asked the top female mammal spotter what motivates her. Karen Baker lives in the south of England, sewing bespoke curtains and traveling as often as she can. "Two things," she said, smiling. "Joy and curiosity." As part of the self-styled Four Amigos, Karen and I did a trip to the Andes, trying for spectacled bear (which we all got) and mountain tapir (which three out of the Four Amigos missed, and let their gnashing of teeth ring loud among the mountaintops). "I just love mammals, have ever since I was a child," Karen said. "I love to watch the behavior, and sometimes animals act so funny it makes me laugh out loud (but not so loud you scare them off). Mammal watching has enabled me to travel to many beautiful places, some a little dangerous that one probably wouldn't go to as a rule. I've been in a few dodgy situations—we were almost attacked by Al-Qaeda once, the army had to protect us with tanks—and my lady friends, they tell me anybody sane would prefer a five-star hotel over leeches and a squat toilet. But to be honest, I could never give it up. It's just too much fun."

In 1975, John Updike wrote a wry *New Yorker* article about chasing a Ross's gull, a slim, pink-breasted gull from the high arctic. Rare even in Alaska, this species strayed to Massachusetts one winter, an event that lit up the phone lines. Birders came from all over, and Updike plays the absurdity of the moment against the crowd's excitement and his own (feigned?) incompetence at trying to pick out the gull in question. In the end, Updike moves past sarcasm to admit that after seeing the bird, he went home—the piece is written in the magazine's requisite *pluralis majestatis*—"with a song in our hearts."

In daily life too rarely do we get to use terms like joy, fun, ecstasy. Almost nothing in my nine-to-nine, Monday-to-Saturday working life is joyful—not a single, mimeographed, HR-coded thing. Maybe I shouldn't let the rest of the world in on this dirty secret, but birding is about beauty, sure, and as Jonathan Franzen says, it's also "a way of connecting with a past in which nature was more whole, not fragmented, not degraded—birds being the most visible indicator of a healthy ecosystem." But even more than those noble things, it's about the dopamine hit when you hook up with the beloved of the moment, the day, the year. A big list means many, many hits of happy juice, getting from here to there. One thinks of the movie *Trainspotting*, when the addicts reflect on the state of their compulsion. What outsiders forget (they say) "is the pleasure of it. Otherwise we wouldn't do it." As Ewan McGregor's character points out, pleasure is key. The junkies may be stupid, but they're not *that* flipping stupid.

When I admitted I once drove nonstop from Southern California to Oregon to see a rustic bunting, I left something out.

What I didn't mention is that I had just gotten *back* from the Oregon border. Then this errant finchling shows up, and my first thought was, *Oh shit, not I-5 again.* But back I went, and I am glad I did—and glad I pushed hard to be there at first light, since the Johnny-come-latelies who had stopped to pee or get coffee all missed it. The rustic bunting put in one brief, sunrise showing and then disappeared for four days. To make it even more Ahab-versus-the-whale, this species and I had history, since I had already missed it twice before. When I finally saw it, did I do the happy dance? Oh baby, you betcha, and trust me, when I dance I am much less graceful than the six-foot-seven poet Charles Olson, whom his student Merce Cunningham once compared to an agile walrus. Still, whoops were whooped and jigs were jiggled, ab-so-effin-lutely. (And then I pulled my truck under some trees and slept for ten hours.)

The trip paid off in other ways. When I left, I had given up ever being able to finish a manuscript, a poetry book called *The Xopilote Cantos*. The title connects a Central American word for vulture with an allusion to Ezra Pound and the desert photographer Richard Misrach. Of course I had a journal with me on that drive; a journal is as essential as binoculars. The brain works however it works, and during the trip, when I saw stars on a moonless night reflect back at me out of a reservoir's obsidian surface, the experience unlocked language and thoughts that completely transformed the end of the book. (I pulled over every fifteen minutes to write things down, then sped on, racing to make up time.) On that long drive I also got to think a lot about how and why some marriages flourish and others don't, about where I wanted to be in five years, and what I was going to do to recalibrate my teaching in the semesters to come.

Couldn't those insights have come at home, eating oatmeal and reading the Sunday paper? Probably not. The dislocation of time and scenery helped, the isolation and intense duration of nonstop thinking, they factored in—and besides, *rustic bunting*. Do you know how good that is for an American bird list? Church bells were ringing, let me tell you.

One area of psychology collects all of this under something called a theory of flow. Flow blends expertise with opportunity in ways often found while listing. As summarized by Joachim Krueger, "In a state of flow, a person is engaged in a challenging task, working away, making progress, while being fully absorbed. Activity and lack of self-consciousness are the key elements of flow." He summarizes work by Mihaly Csikszentmihalyi, who asserts that flow happens when "a person (1) is engaged in a doable task, (2) is able to focus, (3) has a clear goal, (4) receives immediate feedback, (5) moves without worrying, (6) has a sense of control, (7) has suspended the sense of self, and (8) has temporarily lost a sense of time."

Sounds like a good day in the woods to me. Once in Senegal I was with a couple of very fit guys, and we did a twenty-mile walk by accident. We had no goal or destination—we had seen all of our local bird targets, so were just scouting in general what was around. It was the savanna-Sahel transition, meaning low grasses and widely spaced acacia trees, and you could see for miles. There were no lions, bandits, rivers, or villages: we could more or less walk anywhere we wanted. Going hill to hill and talking and stopping to scan with spotting scopes, we finally realized it was nearly midday and we were nine or ten miles from the van. No problem. We each had a long drink of water, shared around a candy bar, took a quick compass bearing, and began to loop our way back on the road. It felt more like floating than walking, as we flowed through the open landscape, unworried about anything.

Lists bend time three ways. There is looking ahead: contemplating the abstract promises of a new site. *Others have seen this there, maybe I will too.* Another is looking back, as you review notes and think about what good (even spectacular) things you've been blessed to have witnessed so far. This has scientific and cultural value; over time, ranges change or species become less common or more so, and day lists and field notes help document that. Mostly what I value is the swat to the backside that makes me attend to the immediacy of the present. First, I need to go out and *have* a "present": be in the interesting place in the first place where sights, sounds, smells, twists of light, quirks of fate, snake-charmed cobras, and tommy-stotting gazelles can be part of my world.

It is easy to mock extremes—the baseline for "extreme" being whatever we ourselves consider normal. For me, stopping to ID roadkill makes perfect sense. How else do I know what's around? In summer, I also keep a snake hook in the back of the truck, because snakes like the midnight warmth of paved roads, and you never know when you'll need to coax a western diamondback out of harm's way. It is just good citizenship. Yet other examples of self-induced fanaticism baffle me completely, such as ultramarathoning, which seems like a good way to ruin both a weekend and a pair of perfectly good trail shoes.

Listing beats doing drugs (there are well over 10,000 species of birds; there are not 10,000 kinds of drugs), and if giving in to the insistent siren of your list means you have to forfeit social niceties, miss the bridal shower (or even the whole wedding itself), so be it, since some priorities rise above others, and while the condor and the black-footed ferret did come back from extinction, other parts of nature may not. Go while you still can. Sooner or later you will be too beat down to travel, too broke or too cranky or too sore or too lonely. Go before the border closes, the crevasse widens, the herd thins, the engine stalls, or the pestilence spreads. Take a friend if you can; go alone if you must.

All birders have their "best of" memories, linked to the times when a chase paid off like a million-dollar hand of black-jack. My most numinous moment comes from the Highlands of Papua New Guinea, side trail off of a side trail in a range so remote many of the children have never before seen a white fellow. (And having met me, they are pretty sure they do not want to see another.) I have been traveling alone, doing ethnographic work. But I have been birding too; no day is too full of chores that you can't still list.

Picturesque village of open-sided, thatched-roof huts on the edge of a giant meadow that washes up like a lake against the blacker, greener wall of primary rainforest. As guest of the headman, I have been invited to stay as long as I wish, and after a tranquil night, I have just stepped out of my hut into cold dawn air. I am struggling to sort the birdcalls by group—parrots, fantails, drongos, pigeons. Too much sound to process; it feels like the soundtrack has been laid down with a hundred channels, and my brain pleads for everybody to slow down and wait their turn. "One noise at a time, please!"

The meadow is part of the Myola grasslands. In most of it, the grass is taller than my head. There was war here once; Americans and Australians fought the Japanese here in World War II, and I had been shown helmets, swords, gun barrels, everything unified under the truce flag of age and rust. The day before I had been taken deep into the forest to see a wrecked plane, a P-40 with white stars on the fuselage and ammunition still fused in the wing guns. *Balus gone pinis*—"the plane is dead," in the simple, declarative phrase of New Guinea pidgin. I hoped the pilot had ejected safely, but there was no way to be sure.

In the village, I can hear everybody waking up. It is going to be an astoundingly beautiful day: the air could not be any more fresh and pellucid. I am smiling as my head swings back and forth, back and forth, tracking the twisting passes of small jet-fighter birds hunting insects in the clean morning light.

These are glossy swiftlets, midnight blue above, though not so much mere blue as an explosion of purples, blues, and blacks, all shimmering with an impossible luminosity. Black wings and black v-notch tail, white belly; but they are not just color, but color plus speed: intensely, hypersonically acrobatic.

And it gets better, my dopey grin going wider and wider, since in hunting at eye level around the huts, the birds have broken the spiderwebs that always appear overnight. As the tallest person in the village, I know these spiderwebs very well: my face is full of them every new dawn. But now somebody else is doing the spider cleaning for me. Blue-black birds are slinging themselves through the air in tight, banking turns, and as they fly, they are breaking cobwebs and trailing them behind them. And as each bird pulls out of the arc and comes around again, long tinsels of cobweb catch the light and flame with incandescence.

Some of the cobwebs are three feet long, and they go invisible as the birds turn against the light, then *bam,* switch back on again.

Listing took me there; beauty that I found there took me to a different place, unexpected and better. We are each a flaming arc of atoms careening through the infinite air, and at that moment, on an offshoot of the Kokoda Trail in a remote part of New Guinea, I could see it, know it, feel it, learn from it.

I am not sure what comes next, but my mammal list is aiming for a glowing number—an even 1,000—and I am leaning hard into it, arms airplaned out full stretch, eyes winced into blue slits against the glare, and I don't want to stop to check, but I sure hope that the rest of my life is following close behind.

/ just saying hello

my blended family is more blended than your blended family

boys don't cry

rhizomes

this one we're not sure about

legbone (borrowed from an ostrich)

heart (in the wrong place)

envy

spite

Domenic Messeri Park yesterday before it got windy

— Say's phoebe
— Black phoebe
— vermilion flycatcher

all on the same fence by the baseball diamond + 35 or more bushtits feeding in the Chinese (?) elms by the skate park (and according to eBird nobody saw it but me)

## CHAPTER 2
# Your Body Is Where You Live

OK fine but what were the names of the horses?

Hy that cake, went to a hos... ↙

1 2 3 4 5 6 7 8 9 10 11 12 13 14 15 16 19 20

# Nature Journals for Fun and Profit

As one might expect of a published nature author, I do keep a journal, but I would like my journal better if it didn't so often remind me of how badly I write, how poorly I draw, how little I notice, and how completely my once-clean Palmer script has devolved into the wild, ink-splattered swings of a faulty seismograph. Ours is a relationship based on suspicion and regret, a failed marriage neither of us has the capacity to leave or change. And unlike most other writers (or at least most writers whose journals have been published), I do not write in complete sentences and narrated dialogue. Instead, I string up a volleyball net across the beach of experience and wait for strange and interesting things to fly into it and stop, trapped and struggling, wondering what went wrong. My pages look less like a diary or business ledger and more like a bug-splattered windshield five hundred miles into a seven-hundred-mile drive.

Not that all the handwriting in my journal is squiggly or bad. It can't be: some of it isn't even mine. That's because I sometimes ask others to draw or write directly in my journal. It works like this. Let's say we're a group of five or six people—witty, cultured, a bit giddy after a full conference day or all of us catching up in London after separate journeys. In my experience, somebody will almost always be the loudest, the most insistent, while a few will be midrange and one will be the shyest. My usual approach is to talk to the quiet one for a while and then take out my journal and offer a trade: I will buy you a drink if you write down the most interesting thing that happened today. This is not about trying to be flirty, nor is it a game of gotcha—I will respect their privacy, and never share anything without permission. I just like the poly-vocality of it all. I already know what I sound like on the page. What does the rest of the world have to say?

Luckily for us, Charles Darwin did believe in sentences and paragraphs as well as taking notes, hence his delightful book *Voyage of the Beagle*. Sea journeys seem to make people write more. After *Moby-Dick*, Herman Melville's notebooks generally only filled up when he was aboard a ship or taking a long trip. In 1857 he went to the Levant, traveling second class to save money and recording everything from prices to the conversation at dinner to the patter of the guides at the main sites. "Here is a stone Christ leaned against, and here is the English Hotel," his guide explained. "That arch is where Christ was shown to the people, right by the window where is the best coffee in Jerusalem."

During his darkest bipolar days, Melville sought out grave-yards and stony fields, leper colonies and funeral processions. After one especially bad night he said he felt "utterly used up," as if "broken on the wheel." Yet even then, irony was a steady rail-ing. Outside Istanbul he noted Roman cemeteries being farmed as ad hoc garden plots. Of Constantine's fallen legions, he said they had been "sowed in corruption & raised in potatoes." My own pilgrimage to Istanbul was more exuberant. Happy to see a new bird in the Bosporus (also known as the Strait of Istan-bul), I used a string of exclamation marks to celebrate a flock of "28 Yelkouan shearwaters!!!" This is basically a Manx shearwater that has been split off into its own Mediterranean species, swift winged and balletic. They are not unexpected here, but for me they were new and marvelous—another marker of exoticism, like seeing a scimitar in a back-alley pawnshop and trying to type on the hotel's computer, fingers hesitant on the Turkish keyboard.

When it comes journaling quantity and ambition, my model is not Melville but Jay Leno. Mr. Leno owns 181 cars and nearly as many motorcycles—the same number as me, except I have amassed that count in journals. They range from elegant, hand-made artists' books to memo pads from Dollar General. They are all nature journals and they are all anti-nature journals;

sometimes I complain about the ants that keep biting me as I am trying to photograph flowers in Arizona, or I paste over a day's dull bird list with the ticket stubs from that night's symphony. Some things are worth remembering and other things, not so much.

Don't tell that to the Transcendentalists. They carried their notebooks everywhere. In the Harvard Press edition, Emerson's journals span sixteen volumes and Henry David Thoreau's collected writings beat that, coming in at an even twenty. Just in Concord alone, Nathaniel Hawthorne kept journals, Hawthorne's wife Sophia Peabody kept journals, abolitionist Bronson Alcott did, Alcott's daughter (and author of *Little Women*) Louisa May did, as did feminist Margaret Fuller, the poet and Unitarian pastor William Ellery Channing, and probably even the town alderman and the dogcatcher's apprentice. Louise May Alcott ate apples while writing in her journal—hers was a vegetarian household. I do that too, but I alternate apples with oatmeal cookies chased by Jack and Coke. I then chastise myself in my journal for my bad habits; like Benjamin Franklin, I keep journals to document my self-improvement, even when there is very little good news to report.

Here's why journals mattered to those grand old American idealists and still matter to me. Our brains are really good at being idea factories, but journals make us smarter by letting us remember how smart we already are. My theory is that we have tidal waves of insight all day long—in fact, I think most of us have a thousand ideas per hour—but if we don't write things down, all those quirky thoughts and clever phrases rush immediately back out to sea, leaving behind a mudflat inhabited only by stunned fish and perplexed regret.

This is not a universally recognized law. My students hate me for many reasons, but being made to keep journals is one of them. The first time we take off our shoes and draw them in our journals, they hate on me *so hard*, it's as if twenty-five little tornadoes of fury are rising above the desks. At least they can't accuse me of hypocrisy, since I draw mine too. And at term's end, when we do the course review, many of them say, "Remember when we drew our shoes? That was so cool!" (They also like using Polaroid cameras to demonstrate examples of thesis and transition, and in the night class, reading Emily Dickinson by candlelight.)

On family trips I always encouraged my children to keep journals, which I have saved to return later. It seems that Hawai'i was especially good for buffets, while in Costa Rica *iguana* was a tricky word to spell; each of the kids came up with a different solution. Male howler monkeys have black fur and blue testicles, so everybody had something to say about that. My daughter and I once watched a courtship *pas de deux* between two rattlesnakes, something I had forgotten until her journal from a San Diego trip reminded us both. She was only ten but had taken good notes.

Looking back, I don't think I was a very good father, but I made sure all my kids could split wood and light a fire from scratch, and that before they started high school they knew how to ride a bike, a horse, and a longboard. When one of the boys started a band, I had a truck, so I became chief roadie. All of my kids were taught how to drive a stick and how to tell a raven from a crow. None of them was ever bitten by a snake. None ever got lost or needed to be helicoptered out of the backcountry. If I remembered to say *I love you* to them, so much the better. With a rash guard and a passport, the world was theirs.

One thing I never had to tell any of them was that weary parental admonition, "Use your words!" When did we start saying that, as a culture? My parents never said it to me and I never said it to my kids, but then there came a time when I seemed to hear new parents everywhere repeating it like a chorus of exhausted frogs. Aw come on, folks, they *are* using their words—tantrums have a syntax that is older than the coelacanth fish. In any case, once I realized I was hearing it daily, I made a note of the date in my journal. Trouble is, writing this, I can't find that entry now. I can see it so clearly in my mind. I would like to share how I have all of my journals archived in a special library at my house, arranged chronologically and always ready for service, but that would be a big fat fib. Most of them are in the guest bedroom along with the high school yearbooks and broken tripods and winter sleeping bags, but a few are in a drawer in my campus office, one or more still in the car, one in the pocket of a daypack, and maybe one or two next to the laptop, depending on which projects are currently cooking. In the end I can usually find what I want, but it takes much longer than it should—*shhh*, speak softly, you'll wake up my guilty conscience. I admire organized people very much and hope one day to join their tribe.

I keep journals to be the bearer of love and memory for the unlovely and unremembered places on the planet. Attend all now this hubcap, this spore print from a mushroom, this postcard from Ely, Nevada. Stand anywhere, draw a circle, know that this circle has been many things to many people since long before you came along. What were the local names for this creek or bush or corner lot, before there were roads and stop signs? When T. S. Eliot promises to show us fear in a handful of dust, all I have to answer is that I can show him cigarette butts and bits of wire in that same dust, but that if you twist the wire into rings and add in a few forks from the dump, you can make crazy fun windchimes.

Some of my journals are to-do lists for a future self, a self of more leisure (and perseverance) than exists now. File this under P (for "Projects Yet to Come"), but my journal reminds me that I want to tell the story of Richard Meinertzhagen, independently wealthy British ornithologist and utter sociopath. (He served with Lawrence of Arabia, who thought he was too savage.)

In East Africa at the start of World War I, Meinertzhagen had dinner with a German officer who did not know war had broken out. After an excellent meal, Meinhertzhagen informed him of the true state of world affairs and shot him on the spot. Later, he stole nineteenth-century museum specimens, relabeled them, and submitted them as evidence to name a new subspecies of redpoll after himself.

I also keep journals to remember smaller, more humble stories. It's not hard to remember my wedding or where I was during major earthquakes, but the small moments—the spilled grains of salt that the mind would otherwise sweep off the table, tidying up—can disappear completely if I don't make note of them. Coming back from Gabon, West Africa, one of my fellow mammal listers was put in charge of the group's rat skulls. These were jungle animals, not wharf rats, and we needed them as voucher specimens for museum scientists. My journal remembers that I asked our designated smuggler how he would get them through customs. "Oh, I will put each one inside two condoms and put those inside my UN first aid kit. They never check there."

Good to know.

On the same journey we found a chimpanzee skull in an unvisited part of the forest. No body, just the head. Nobody wanted to touch it; it looked too much like the remains of a decapitated child. We took a picture and left it where it was.

Apparently, one day in Istanbul I spent the morning at the "Church of Push and Trample," then read Melville and had a bowl of spumoni. Somewhere that day there was a turtledove; another place, a black-and-white-winged bird called a hoopoe. Where and why? That didn't get written down. I also now wonder what made me want to remember that I had a conversation with a French boy who had "white pants, peach-colored polo, and a Tony Curtis smile." His hands "fluttered like paper napkins blowing off a table."

That's why I never travel without a pocket notebook, not even to go to church or the store. Anytime I am in an especially supercharged environment—an art museum, a big-time public lecture, any hike longer than ten minutes—then for sure I have a full-sized journal with me. I am one of those dad-nerds who wears a fanny pack turned around facing front; I want my hands free to raise binoculars but want the notebook close at hand to write down what I have just seen. (All my journals have bite marks in the corners from where I clamped the book in my mouth to free up my hands.)

My journal wants me to know everything—to know more than Wikipedia or a boatload of Talmudic scholars, more than all the topics argued over while passing the bottle in all the late-night bull sessions in all the field stations in the world. Did you know that Florida's manatees sometimes swim to Cuba? If not, now you do: from my journal to yours, sent with love. There are twenty species of elephant shrew, and nobody has seen them all. Aardvark meat tastes like beef. The tamandua anteater's mouth is no bigger around than a pencil. That Nazi plane in *Raiders of the Lost Ark*, the flying wing, was based on an obscure yet real prototype, designed in 1943. The real one had jet engines, not propellers, but then you couldn't behead the bad guy.

*The sky is a silent angel dragging her hem in the mud, and we humans just chase after, a scattering of stray sequins and lost beads.*

Why did I write that in my journal, late at night on a bus?

No idea.

What will I do with it?

No idea.

Doesn't matter. It will have a purpose (some distant day). Like a jay, I hoard thousands of acorns, burying them in the mud for later. You should too. Write down one good sentence—your own or somebody else's—and who knows, others may join it. Lyn Hejinian: "The aphorist applies a paddle to a sentence and then leans back to enjoy its drift."

As a reader and writer who tries to be a better reader, better writer, another reason I keep journals is to have a place to celebrate words. Today's entry: *Absquatulate*, to run away (in battle) or to make off with something (jewel heist). I especially love watching natural history terms evolve. "Before they were goatsuckers, nightjars were fern-owls," or so explains a British history of ornithology. *Ablation* means one thing in glacier studies and another in heart surgery; my notes cover both. I once studied poetry with Louise Glück, who later got the Nobel Prize. From her poem "Mock Orange," I once copied out this opening stanza:

> It is not the moon, I tell you.
> It is these flowers
> lighting the yard.

Turning two pages past that, I find more entries for what I call the poetics of work, since logging camps (I wrote down) have gandy dancers, choke setters, knuckle boomers, and cat skinners.

If colors intoxicate artists, language intoxicates me. In oil fields and on offshore derricks, a ginzel is the lowest ranking worker—ranked even below a worm. A finger has been in the field long enough to not be a worm, but is not yet experienced enough to be considered a hand. Dog-House: a room on the drill floor containing the Knowledge Box.

I don't know about you, but I covet working anyplace that has a dedicated knowledge box. I might have called my old faculty office that, but I've been relocated to a trailer, and since my one-thousand-book poetry library could not come with me, I donated it to a rival MFA program.

So many great words, it's hard to keep up. "Ginzel" reminds me of John Muir's favorite bird, the water ouzel. (It walks on the bottoms of streams and is now more commonly called the dipper.) That in turn echoes a European weed, common in Northern California, the teasel (also spelled teazel). Language doesn't only limit itself to the clean and the sober, and so I take my jazzy, woozy, swoon-inducing words wherever I can find them, even in the sadness of current events. A journal page from a few months ago documents the fact that street names for codeine include Captain Cody and Doors-and-Fours. Fentanyl goes by Jackpot and Apache and China White, but also by my favorite term of all, Tango and Cash (Sylvester Stallone and Kurt Russell, 1989; long may they reign).

We know that drawing and writing help train attention. To quote sixteen-year-old naturalist Fiona Gillogly, who learned nature journaling from her friend John Muir Laws, "The more interested you are in something, the more interesting it becomes." That fact motivates me, certainly. You can see it in action in their nature journals, and also in those of the British artist Jo Brown, whose *Secrets of a Devon Wood* makes her the Jack Laws of England. The other day I was in a nearby dirt lot, doing one of those "describe all the objects in a ten-meter radius" projects that help one learn one's local ecology, and it really was true: the longer I spent, the more I found. Some of it was cultural—vintage barbed wire, modern to-go cups, and everything in between—but a lot of it was nature I had overlooked, included the tremendous quantity of desiccated jackrabbit pellets that cover just about every square inch of soil. It must take them years to break down into dust and beetle kibble. (If horse droppings are road apples, should these be called desert dingleberries?)

To be honest, at some level I also keep journals out of fear. What if language abandons me? I watched my father disappear into the inexorable fogbank of Alzheimer's, and know my turn will come sooner or later. Once I start to lose language, once I cannot follow the ever-thinning threads of narrative and meaning, I pretend to myself that this handwritten cache of words will still be here, if not to save me, then at least to give me a few final meals before the long, hard winter to come.

Where can my heart go to flee from my heart? I have to admit that I can be deeply evasive in journals. I observe nature daily but write about feelings rarely, and if I am thinking about something dark like suicide—not often, but true and real when it is present, like a stranger on the train you keep staring at, sure you've seen him somewhere before—those journal passages become so oblique and encrypted that I intend for nobody in my family to be able to penetrate them. Our most private parts of our bodies are our minds, and for me, I prefer to keep the shades drawn and the doors locked. What is that substance that has astronomers so flummoxed, *dark matter*? The greatest constellations may coalesce out of the parts of the sky we cannot see.

Dear journal: RuPaul was right, I *am* God in drag.

Dear journal: When was the last time I looked like anybody in the Patagonia catalogs?

Dear journal: Do me a favor and erase the bad pages, the self-pitying ones, the ones that I wish would disappear, like those magic stones you paint on with water and the writing goes from black to gray to nothing at all, three minutes, two minutes, no minutes.

Dear journal, I knew somebody who almost became a ginzel. It turned out differently for him, and for me, too; I went to school in the humanities instead of following my hero, Red Adair, somebody who puts out fires on oil derricks and who in *Hellfighters*, 1968, is played by John Wayne.

Dear journal, macho movies sometimes ignite legitimate dreams.

Dear journal, then again, maybe not.

Dear journal, when I was growing up my father kept his spare life in a shed—his spurs, his boots, his lariat, two bridles, a new hat still in a box. What movies was he playing in his head? It was like he was not part of the family and was just here visiting. At night, when bored, he would go around and turn off the lights while the rest of us were still up, just to hear the commotion.

One my stories about him is this. After the Second World War my father was hitchhiking from San Diego to Oklahoma, thinking maybe he could be a roustabout in the oilfields. He had served in the Atlantic and the Pacific, on ships that had been shot at by U-Boats and dive-bombed by the Japanese, so he was ready to turn his back on the sea. Everybody hitchhiked back then—that is one thing Kerouac got right in *On the Road*—and a truck loaded with alfalfa picked him up. But it was not going to Oklahoma; it was headed into the Superstition Mountains by way of Queen Valley and Superior, and did he want to come? He said sure, why not, and that truck took him to a ranch in Arizona which was short a few men. My father became a cowhand instead of a driller, running Angus and Herefords, living in log cabins. Rope and horse, no gun. Just another working guy, worn leather gloves and a sunburned squint. In the few photos I have from then, he looks like Gary Cooper.

I once asked my father if it's true, can horses sleep standing up.

"Yes, it is," he said, "and in fact I had this one horse, right after the war, it could sleep while walking."

"Can people sleep standing up?"

"Well, the blankets fall off."

"But can they."

"Sure, you lean on the wall, lock your knees. With practice you don't need the wall. Just stand in the middle of the snow, sleeping. Don't even need a tent. That's how we won the Battle of the Bulge when we were fighting Hitler. Middle of winter. Our guys travelled through the forest like Mohicans and when they wanted to rest, two or three stood back to back. Half would sleep a few hours while the other half kept lookout."

Sometimes we had these kinds of conversations. Other times he had flare-ups of anger and a strange need to blame me when things went south. And then there are my sad, shame-filled memories of him sitting alone in the dark, on the steps leading up to our apartment, how there was nothing to see but his lean jaw and the red glow of his cigarette. Was he remembering the cattle country, regretting Los Angeles? I remember looking at him across the table like I was eating dinner with a stone God on loan from Easter Island. (Later when I went to the real Easter Island, I thought they had not gotten him quite right—they made all the statues too small.)

When I first began to publish my writing, hesitatingly, and unsure of voice or subject, I think he always found my writing a bit effeminate, a bit of a disappointment. He liked writers like O. Henry and Zane Grey, to name two people I will never be. When I was rock climbing a lot, that was fine, but then came birdwatching and studying flowers and writing poetry books: in his eyes, I might as well have gotten a tattoo on my forehead that said "homosexual."

Such a cliché, isn't it, the lonely child finding solace in nature.

Find it I did, drawing animals at the zoo, catching ladybugs in the corner lot and pollywogs in the Los Angeles River. A friend of my parents, somebody now ascended into the heavenly ante-chamber of back-in-the-day lost-ness, paid me fifty cents for a tableau drawn in marker on a continuous strip of bedsheet. The scene, set in East Africa, recreated an entire hunting pageant. There were lions, zebras, a rhino, a herd of impalas, and in all I had tried to create a veldt version of the Bayeux Tapestry, but with way more teeth and blood.

Normally I never would have parted with such a treasure, but as they say, cash is king.

As my circles widened, my journals kept up. Hitchhiking in Alaska. Working with sea turtles in Baja. Solar eclipse, Costa Rica. And then finally reaching the continent of Africa itself, the first of almost a dozen trips.

My journals span all the octaves. I do have dark pages, true, but for every dark page there is a light one, and on whole, the light ones outnumber the grim ones ten to one. That is good to know, to see, looking back on them now. This passage is from one of the African trips, as I was leaving Senegal to cross back into Gambia. Somebody please carve the last sentence onto my headstone.

"Left before first light. Long-tailed nightjars, plovers, goats, barn owls, scrub hares on the road; men in blue turbans, then a dead donkey, then a row of baobabs like a Greek temple made out of oversized bowling pins. Ferry back across the River Gambia: pink-backed pelicans nesting in trees and then unexpected and unexplained, an immense butterfly migration a mile wide and ten miles tall—huge, dispersed river of butterflies going upstream along the river course, far as eye can see, up and up, taller than the sky. Resting on my back on the deck to focus upwards in layers, fifty feet, a hundred feet, two hundred feet—all the way up to the top reach of the Zeiss binoculars, butterflies all the way up. Aliou looks pleased when I tell him, but it turns out, his sly smile is not about that, but about what he has learned, calling ahead. He tells me the rumor is that when we get to the lodge we're having 'triple good' for dinner, and when I don't understand, he explains it is going to be not one but three: wart hog ('bush pig'), peanut stew, and goat curry. Drawing in close to shore we can see mudskipper fish wiggle-darting in the shallows around the mangrove roots. Vultures sulk on snags. The diesel fumes smell like dad's truck. Hot today but good. I am happy. I am so very, very happy."

# Fifty Dreams for Forty Monkeys

1. Shrink Los Angeles so it fits inside a snow globe, then shake it. The dots won't be white. Not snowflakes—when does it ever snow in Los Angeles?—but swirling specks of red and green, hundreds of them, hundreds and hundreds of vivid green dots.

2. Each dot is a parrot. Shake it and watch them fill the sky. Parrots also fill the domes of Bakersfield, San Francisco, La Jolla, and even the well-tended, richly treed grounds of the Getty Villa in Malibu. Temple City. Altadena. Most of Southern California, one way or another, and plenty of other places. Phoenix? Yes, even Phoenix.

3. "Parrots" means parrots, but also everybody else: lorries, conures, budgies, red-crowned Amazons, yellow-chevroned parakeets, and even the occasional and very expensive blue-and-gold macaw. Parrots means the collective tribe of psittacines who generally live in jungles, and generally have green

bodies and red heads (lots of variation there, of course), and generally make a screechy racket streaking around overhead, and generally like big, tall, exotic trees like the silk-floss tree, but which pretty much never met a tree they didn't like, from native sycamores to feral pomegranates.

4. Call them exotics, they don't mind. Call them anything you want, really.

5. People love pets; people love parrots as pets; people are stupid; from llamas to pit bulls, pets get loose; among the things that get loose, it makes sense that parrots got loose / get loose (past tense and continuing present tense); years ago all those loose parrots started to find each other and form chattering parrot gangs; and on Saturday night when the daddy parrot loves the mommy parrot very, very much then they make baby parrots, and then as teenagers, those once-baby parrots get drunk at prom and have babies of their own, and now some of the free-flying, baby-making, sky-screeching feral parrot species number in aggregates of hundreds, even thousands of individuals.

6. And not just parrots.

7. In the long list of introduced birds, watch for bishops, bulbuls, mannikins, waxbills, whydahs, and white-eyes.

8. And not just birds.

9. All hail the flowerpot snake, small and blind, and beware the dreaded coquí frog, coming to ruin a night's sleep some-

where near you. And listen for a modest, cricket-like *chirp* from the Mediterranean house gecko. Where did they come from? Oh, a pet store probably, or a houseplant somebody shouldn't have imported, or they got trapped in a crate of macadamia nuts. All of the above, none of the above. Who knows. How did *you* get here?

10. Besides parrots, besides geckos, what other things have I seen sold in pet stores? If I think back as far as I can remember it becomes a sad and infinite list, because I can remember seeing for sale—seeing with my own eyes, here in America—chipmunks, skunks, ocelots, squirrel monkeys, gibbons, chimpanzees.

11. Admittedly, this is all back in the day, but while I am old, I am not *that* old.

12. And the pet trade still carries on today, albeit more clandestinely and with a higher profit margin for the really rare stuff.

13. The escapees create complicated feelings in many of us. Birders often hate on starlings and exotics, won't count them on their lists and speak as harshly of them as Trump does of immigrants. Yet I must say, when it comes to starlings, they *are* snappy looking birds, aren't they? Just considered objectively, they are worth appreciating for their plumage and their willingness to make a living even in the middle of our very busy cities.

14. Because the thing is, I live when I live, and while I can yearn for the passenger pigeon or the truly stupendous and entirely

extinct Carolina parakeet, that won't help me get through the day. I have to love what the day allows me to love, and my days include—for better or worse but they do—plumped-up little balls of starling-ness in the morning sunshine on the tops of my neighbor's Italian (I think?) cypress, and when the light catches them, oh how they shine.

15. Margaret Millar: "Occasionally I am asked what difference bird watching has made in my life. I can only repeat, the days don't begin quickly enough, and never last long enough, and the years go by too soon."

16. Memory of childhood, happy and indelible: I was on vacation with my family, we were at a zoo (maybe Portland, Oregon?), a gang of squirrel monkeys had gotten loose somehow and were free-roaming on the zoo grounds. The thrill, in those innocent and presexual days, my thrill in coming across these seemingly wild monkeys, oh my gosh, it was like being filled with five hundred volts of electricity. I can taste it still, feel it, remember it. Just about the best thing ever.

17. Am I a bad birder to admit that on my expeditions to the Amazon, I like seeing monkeys even more than I like seeing wild parrots? *Like* as a word may be too brief, too shallow. LOVE in block caps, that's closer. I *love* seeing wild monkeys, as does my wife; it is one of her favorite nature things, and as she says, "Monkeys—*they have people fingers.*"

18. Henri Rousseau called them his "Mexican paintings," the exotic jungle landscapes he conjured up, like the one that has a chain of monkeys linked up hand to foot to shake oranges

out of a swan-winged tree. Flowers, foliage, and monkeys fill the canvas; there is hardly room for the sky, which sits on the top of forest like a forgotten hanky. Rousseau implied he based these scenes on what he had seen in military service abroad, but in actuality he made them all in Paris, and they were just versions of the zoo and botanical gardens and illustrated magazines, garden plants taken in by his generous heart and scaled up ten-fold. It works, though: The paintings *read* like jungles and monkeys, and you know that if he had found a spider monkey sitting at his table one morning, he would not have been surprised at all. He would have halved a grapefruit and shared it over, and he and the monkey would have eaten toast and read *Le Figaro* in companionable silence.

19. Ages ago when I was a docent at San Joaquin Marsh in Orange County, there was talk about the Alligator of Back Bay. For three years it evaded capture. Not truly an alligator: in the end, it turned out to be a spectacled caiman, native to South America. Locals called it Wally. But it was five feet long and terrorizing the mullet. (It also supposedly ate coots and opossums.) Discussions circulated among the staff about what to do if we saw it, how it could be captured. It usually lived in Upper Newport Bay, but also ranged upstream in the creek that ran past the marsh and UC Irvine. It all sounded rather jolly to me; I hoped to see it myself, and doubted it was having all that much impact. It was just doing what its nature told it to do: live in an estuary and eat whatever it could catch. It probably took out fewer raccoons per week than were killed by cars speeding on University Drive. Before that, there was a capybara (largest rodent in the world) loose in Orange County, and even a contingent of Marines from

Camp Pendleton couldn't track it down. I found that amusing as well. Wildlife: 1, humans: nil, and if I am betting on the long-term results, my money is on the wildlife.

20. Of course, it is bad (*very bad*) to release pets into nature. Do not ever do it.

21. That said, I do wish—secretly but fervently—I wish that the same careless dolts who let their parrots escape had accidentally let their pet squirrel monkeys escape too. Not hundreds, but enough so that they could have met up, formed a self-sustaining colony. Can you imagine the thrill of it? How utterly supercalifragilisticexpialidocious it would be if you were by Golden Gate Park or the LA River, if you were out birding or walking the dog or doing a slow, struggling, five-mile run, and suddenly you came across a frisky, scampering troupe of thirty or forty squirrel monkeys, feral and happy and chittering excitedly as they raided an abandoned orange tree.

22. Because that's why parrots do so well: fruit. Not just citrus, but exotic fruit more generally. All the off-the-charts tropical landscaping makes for a year-round, lavish abundance of fruit. If we can support thousands of wild parrots and not feel a burden (and we can), why then not feral monkeys too? Not big kinds, they might bite or fling poo; but some species of marmosets are small as hamsters—their ecological footprint wouldn't be much bigger than that of LA's introduced fox squirrels.

23. To repeat, it is bad, very bad, to release pets into nature. *Do not do it.*

24. But if you were going to do it...

25. No, *bad*. It is bad to introduce nonnative species into any ecology, even an urban one.

26. Some species introduction stories have surprise endings. Los Angeles had a bird from Asia that is mostly but not entirely gone, the spotted dove, which looks like a regular mourning dove but with an added back-of-nape black bandana speckled with white stars. Common as all get-out, once upon a time. Here one day, seemingly permanently so, and then, suddenly—*whoosh*, they all disappeared.

27. Happens all the time. Some introductions fail. Most do, in fact, and that is a good thing. (They don't fail often enough.) One bird that seemed to be established in the New World was the crested myna, native to Asia. Wayne Weber, from a thread on the bird forums: "The history of crested mynas in North America is interesting. They were first reported around Vancouver in 1897, and the last ones were seen in 2003. In other words, they were present for at least 106 years. The population was estimated to be about 20,000 at one time, and they spread as far as the outer limits of the Vancouver metropolitan area." Yet now they are gone. Vancouver is a myna-free zone. Other myna sites have replaced it, and since 1997, the birds have been present in Lisbon, Portugal, so far doing fine. What makes one population able to linger while other populations die out? No clear pattern reveals itself.

28. At the end of Werner Herzog's hallucinatory movie about the Spanish Conquest, *Aguirre, the Wrath of God*, the titular

character gives a final soliloquy to a crazed horde of squirrel monkeys. He does this in rusty armor, floating down the Amazon, while his daughter and final companions sprawl around him, dying on their moss-covered, barely intact bamboo raft. How did a movie made with a stolen camera and barely enough money for rice and beans ever afford an animal wrangler and four hundred trained monkeys? Answer: well, they didn't afford it because they couldn't. They were filming in the jungle, so Herzog hired a local trapper to round up some wild monkeys, all of which they would release after the day's shooting. Fine, except the trapper double-crossed him and tried to export the monkeys to the great and grand US of A, a country where we have a bottomless appetite for mahogany, tequila, cocaine, looted Mayan artifacts, and all manner of exotic pets. Remember that the exotic pet trade was legal up until the 1990s. Herzog found out about it and raced to the airport. He pretended to be the regional medical officer, and began screaming in outrage. These monkeys! They had not been vaccinated! Everybody who tried to handle them was at tremendous risk! He must confiscate them all, RIGHT NOW. After he retrieved the monkeys, filming continued. The monkeys survived. You can see for yourself: released on the raft, they all promptly swam back to the flooded forest, aside from a few inadvertent movie stars who for sixty seconds were on the receiving end of the mad ravings of the famously mad Klaus Kinski.

29. Squirrel monkeys are adorably small and nimble, with long tails and a scampering gait, hence the name. They pee on their hands to mark territory.

30. If I were a monkey, I might very well prefer Los Angeles to my native jungle. In the Philippines there is a bird called the monkey-eating eagle. What does it eat? Ah, hmm, yes. It does not occur in California though. And in the South American jungle, there is the harpy eagle, and it takes things as large as a sloth, so a baby monkey, that is no problem at all. Meanwhile, California's native peregrine falcons mostly eat birds—pigeons, ducks, seagulls—so no threat there, while the golden eagle is an open-country bird, so is not going to be hanging around Brentwood waiting to snack on a golden lion tamarin. Cooper's hawks zip among the urban trees nailing robins and juncos, and they hope to pick off the random squirrel or two as well, but trying to snatch dinner by stooping a gang of monkeys? I don't think they would take that risk. Bobcats hunt on the ground and specialize in rabbits, so they don't factor. In the end, urban monkeys might thrive, and I can imagine a scenario where in the same urban tree one could see feeding parrots, feeding warblers, and feeding squirrel monkeys. (Be still my beating heart.)

31. Some introductions are not benign. An escaped tiger lived outside Los Angeles once, giving even the mountain lions reason to flinch. Vaqueros reported tracks the size of dinner plates. It had been an illegal pet and it lived wild until it was seen by somebody in their backyard and was tracked down and shot near an elementary school.

32. If tigers are too much of a good thing, mountain lions seem about the right size, and everybody loves the fact that P-22 made Griffith Park its home. The famous puma crossed multiple freeways to end up in an island of habitat between

Hollywood and the Los Angeles River. In Mumbai, official population thirteen million, wild leopards live inside the city limits, and they eat dogs mostly, and manage to carry on year after year. Nobody knows how many live there—one Indian biologist told me he guessed about three hundred— and when I asked him, "How did they get there?" He just shrugged. "They were always there."

33. All the things in the dark we never notice or think about. What a list that would be.

34. And just as long, a list of the things we wait until dark to do.

35. "Draw me your map of utopia and I'll tell you your tragic flaw," says Laurie Penny.

36. That's okay, as I have many tragic flaws, and at the head of the list is an unreasonable hunger for interesting aesthetic experiences. Animals in trees provide that.

37. Historically, California had zero native parrots, or at least none that we know about, but adjacent New Mexico and Arizona did: the thick-billed parrot, generally considered a Mexican species but one that ranged north to Flagstaff. It was nomadic and/or irruptive, following pinecone crops. Mostly gone now. Circumstantial evidence suggests it was kept as a pet by the Pueblo Indians in the Southwest, who also raised captive macaws, received via trade from Mexico, whose feathers had ceremonial value. This lasted more than a thousand years; macaws were kept from 300 to 1450 CE, and

it makes sense that at least once in a while some got away, living out their lives in New Mexican forests.

38. Recent attempts to reestablish the thick-billed parrot in Arizona didn't work out (too few birds, too many hungry hawks) but a stray—perhaps genuinely wild—thick-billed parrot showed up in New Mexico in 2004. Let the lists swell with joy.

39. To think about the urban jungle is to admit that humans destroy habitat but humans also create habitat, and to discount what I call blended ecologies (part-indigenous, part-cloud cuckoo land) would be like refusing to eat Tex-Mex because it lacks haute cuisine pedigree. Thomas Keller never served fajitas for Christmas dinner, but in my house we're big fans. Out with the old, in with the new, and somebody pass the Cholula.

40. Which brings us to a central problem in wildlife management. On paper, restoration ecology sounds like a noble profession. The hidden gotcha is, restored back to what state? What year do we use as baseline—1950? 1850? 1500?

41. Meanwhile, it may seem impossible, but the birdiest place in all of North America, at least during spring migration, is Los Angeles County. Not Florida, not Alaska, not Monterey. In a single weekend, in a nation-wide competition, Los Angeles County ends up with the most bird species tallied—often surpassing 270 species. As a site, it can cheat in the sense that it has a mountain range *and* a desert, but it also has

something on the order of twenty million people driving sixty million cars or whatever, and so to achieve multiple hundreds of bird species in one weekend, finger snaps for the collective productivity of urban jungles, vacant lots, stony ridges, and muddy culverts.

42. So instead of trying to resurrect an imagined state of lost purity, we might do better to take blended nature at face value. If we say to ourselves, "Okay, this is where we're at: we have x percent native, y percent exotics; what do we have to work with?" we not only might do some good for a certain percentage of species, but I think we could also find some optimism in these days that seem suspiciously like end times for much of life on earth.

43. Aren't these the end times?

44. Not according to all the parrots I saw yesterday.

45. Not according to the coyote pack celebrating the poodle they just brought down.

46. Not according to the leopards of Mumbai and not according to the raccoons who now live in golf courses around Palm Springs and not according to P-22, the ghost king of Griffith Park. Does anybody remember that he used to go into the LA Zoo at night, have a look around? One night he snatched a koala from the Australia exhibit, bounded out of the pen, and ate it. (Does koala meat taste like cough drops?)

47. There are four hundred species of monkey in the world, and another four hundred species of parrot. Some of the parrot species we have already wiped out, permanently and inexorably. Some we have saved. Some live in our cities. Maybe in each lifetime we get no more nature than we deserve, and in that case, shame on us, shame on our fathers before us. But it is not too late: We can make better choices now, a minute from now, in ten minutes. We can always make better choices. *It is not too late.*

48. Camille Dungy: "Ask me if I speak for the snail and I will tell you / I speak for the snail."

49. If the insidious message of capitalism is You're alone; you're not good enough; be worried, be fearful, then the default message from a parrot flock is, Dress loud, make noise, and tell everybody to meet at the silk-floss tree—Mom's not home and ain't nobody gonna call the cops.

50. At night my dreams flare red and green, and each day when I wake up, I look out the window and there it is again, brighter, more saturated: a tree, a flower, a squirrel, a cloud, the shadows of leaves applauding against the driveway, the one dandelion I forgot to weed, the subtle jostle that could be a passing box truck or a train or a very minor earthquake or maybe just the dome of the globe inhaling to fill itself with light, ready for another day of crescendo and shine.

# Two Thousand Palm Trees

I have decided to be reincarnated as a palm tree. That creates a new problem, namely deciding which kind. So many: ivory, peach, cabbage, toddy, petticoat, parlor, king, queen. Wine and sago and fishtail. Two thousand species of palm occur in the wild, though in America almost all of our street palms are exotics, schlepped from not-here to here by ambition or accident until they now feel as natural and inevitable as sushi rolls and pork belly tacos.

History locates palms as far back as we can squint. Tutankhamun's tomb included baskets of doum palm fruit; this is an African species and one of the rare multibranched palms. (Running guns in Ethiopia, Rimbaud slept under a canopy of doum.) Bottle palm is also called Buddha palm, while date palm is mentioned more than any other fruit-bearing plant in the Quran. A row of potted palms indoors once conjured visions of harems and hookahs and tropical living, which is why forty palm trees sank with the *Titanic*.

The palm trees in Hollywood originated in faith, since Mexican fan palms were first carried from Sonora to Alta California to provide fronds for Palm Sunday mass. Palms make multiple cameos in the Bible, such as in Exodus 15:27: "Then they came to Elim, where there were twelve springs and seventy palm trees, and they camped there near the water." The padres did not care that we already had a native palm, California fan palm, tucked into folds in the desert canyons—that kind was too far away, too hard to get to.

With Mexican independence, colonial outreach changed, and by the 1830s the mission settlements in Alta California had been abandoned. By the 1860s, Los Angeles was in gringo hands, but now what? With the transcontinental railroads on their way, time to turn adobe and chaparral into a Destination, capital D. In popular imagination, the rows of orange groves and the midwinter rose parades promised new beginnings and labor-free profits, and so the boosters made use of what was ready at hand. In brochures, the palm-shaded streets came to be stand-ins for the promise of vernal paradise. *There is no winter*, newcomers were promised. *There is no poverty or slums. The oranges will grow themselves, pick themselves, pack themselves in tissue-lined boxes with smiling girls on the labels.* A one-way train ticket was only $5. Print up the handbills, wake up the card sharks: the rubes are coming to town.

Somehow the hustle became the reality. The new people might have been tricked into grubstaking a spiky, fire-prone wilderness, but once here, they came, they saw, they planted. "In a landscape where nothing officially exists (otherwise it would not be 'desert'), absolutely anything becomes thinkable, and may consequently happen"—Reyner Banham. Most arrivals had grown up in towns where planting trees was part of civic pride, or else they remembered childhood farms, where each cluster of houses and barns was centered on the landscape by shade trees and fruit trees, or by a row of trees planted as windbreaks. They knew in the mind's eye what it should look like, but they had to work with what was on hand. Magnolias were expensive, oaks take fifty years to get going, but blue gum eucalyptus was fast and cheap, and mature palm trees could be pilfered from the now-abandoned missions, free for anybody with a shovel and a pony cart. This was a culture that by 1910 could support ten ostrich farms just in Southern California alone. Palm trees were bound to be popular.

Horizons silhouetted by palm trees repeat the lie: *you can never be too tall or too thin.* It is a coveted look, and now fan palms (and the other common species, Canary Island date palm) can be found in San Francisco, in Napa and Sonoma, even in Seattle and Vancouver. Hope and longing flow south too, and fan palms and canary palms follow each other down the coasts of Peru and

Chile, hopscotching from Hollywood all the way to Patagonia.

It was an especially Victorian thing to plant palm trees. John Muir married into money, and when his father-in-law passed, he and his wife moved into the patriarchal mansion in Martinez. It had red wallpaper and lots of bright woodwork; Muir's father-in-law's palm trees still guard the entrance to this day. Their fronds' green glow fills the upstairs windows. When Disney bought the citrus orchard that became Disneyland, as part of the conditions of the sale he had to promise to preserve the Dominguez Tree, a Canary Island palm dating from 1896. It had been a wedding present, and the land's owners didn't want Mr. Disney to desecrate it. He so agreed. The tree is still there; you can see it while waiting in line for the Jungle Boat ride.

Rich people need the reassurance of palm trees just as much as the middle class. Mexican fan palms encircle the hilltop at San Simeon, aka Hearst Castle, aka Xanadu. Hearst had to have them there—how would you know you were in an antechamber of Heaven without a row of paradise-signifying palm trees to mark your arrival?

Palm tree as vision. Drive around long enough and sooner or later you will pass a palm tree on fire with nobody to notice or care, nobody besides yourself. Middle of the night, a flaming top of a palm tree will be sticking up eye-level with the freeway, hardly any smoke, no fire trucks, no helicopters, perfect and indelible, just *there*: a burning palm tree. It might be arson, it might be lighting or firecrackers, it might be a case of spontaneous combustion. You are driving, you see it, and then you will be past it, gone, done, over. No explanation, just a vision of pure orange, intense and magical, burning in the night sky. That is when you know with utmost certainty: *Yes, I am one of the Elect.*

From above, a palm resembles an old toothbrush or a broken umbrella. I once hired a helicopter so I could photograph the Los Angeles River. It was easy to arrange. A friend recommended company x, based at Long Beach Airport. I was nearby, giving a paper at a conference, so I called them up. "Can you guys take the doors off the helicopter?" They answered sure, no problem. I was shocked; I had expected a lecture on safety.

"Wait, you can? *Really?*"

"Yup. Do it all the time."

"Is there a pilot available right now?"

"Yes."

"Do you take credit cards?"

"Of course."

"I'll be there in ten minutes."

We lifted off then hovered in place as the pilot put on his seat belt, having been scolded by the control tower. We swung over to the river's mouth and followed the concrete upstream towards Dodger Stadium and Atwater. One surprise of many: how quickly palm trees became lost in the general static of "city." Compared to regular plants, a palm tree is not much more than a tent pole, a horizon breaker, a prop best seen from ground level, isolated against the clean backdrop of beach or sky. Jared Farmer, who wrote a comprehensive survey of trees in California, reminds us that like "programmed music in a shopping mall, palms perform commercial work on a subliminal level." Indeed, so ubiquitous are they as filler in urban landscaping they're almost invisible, even from the ground.

Fan palms have a small, dense root ball, but I have decided to change that. When I come back reincarnated as a palm tree, I am going to start a new tradition, the taproot tradition, and as tall and vertical as a given palm's trunk is, there will be a corresponding central root stalk drilling straight down into the earth. Rocks, sewer lines, dry soil or wet, I don't care. Moles, move over. Worms, give it up. In my way of running the botanical world, palm trees will have a mirrored life underground, as vertical below grade as they are above the surface. They will anchor the cool sky to the hot core of the earth, holding the world together. Why doesn't everything just fly apart, fragments flung out to space by the tremendous energy of centrifugal force? I have grown up with a lifetime of cruel, superficial untruths about the plastic people in Los Angeles in particular, and California more generally. None of it is true, of course, and if you want to look for great art, interesting theater, top birding, try starting on the West Coast. So yes, myths and misconceptions, plus the swirls and eddies of language from California Indian to Spanish to English and back again to Spanish. History and desire, palm trees watching over each phase. I can't help but hold it together—*I love this city so much*—and when fires and earthquakes and all the plagues yet to come want to ruin things, there will be a force suturing the above-ground lives to the below-ground lives, the living to the dead, able to pull it all back into a unified whole.

Twelve years old and flocking Christmas trees behind a florist's shop: my first paid job, spraying pine trees clumpy white under the bemused gaze of eternal fan palms. Dirty work, asbestos work, but of course I had been given gloves, apron, respirator—*not*. By high school, mowing lawns and raking leaves, I learned to buy good gloves and keep a hacksaw in the car as a fast way to section palm fronds, so they fit in trash bins with room for grass and weeds. Even now I sometimes look up at those toothy fronds and think, *You want to cut me, cut me BADLY, but I won't let you.* Will they even last long enough to be a threat to the next generation of arborists? Some sources suggest that the palm trees of Los Angeles are now at the ends of their lives. Palms are not bristlecones or sequoias; they cannot live forever. I am not convinced the end is upon us (and them) just yet. We do not have good baseline data. How they behave in nature is not well known, and even less is known about the endurance of urban palm trees.

Maybe I just need the visual horizon to last a bit longer because I fear the complete erasure of any world I can recognize. Already the five-and-dimes of childhood are gone, and Sol the butcher. The camera store where we took the vacation slides to be developed is gone. Around the top of the room, just under the ceiling, were three-foot-wide backlit displays of Kodachrome vacation scenes, some of them shot by Ansel Adams, though I didn't know it at the time. Who needs reality if you have film that good? Palm tree love: my parents met in Hollywood— schoolmarm June, say hello to handsome veteran Gene, currently wrangling hosses for the studios—and as a family (brother and me now included), we all went to church in Hollywood, First Hollywood Presbyterian, red brick Gothic Revival surrounded by fan palms. My memory always associates prostitutes with palm trees, women glimpsed out the car window—the first people I learned to identify with bad words above their heads like thought bubbles. Whatever sex was, it had a short skirt and cast long shadows. Driving home from church I saw my first gay men, my first antiwar protestors, my first wino (a new word to me) urinating against a palm tree, and doing it, as my mother said in disgust, "in broad daylight and everything."

Palm trees and desire, desire and memory, the world slipping away from us as we age like a long roll of ribbon you don't know has gotten caught by the bumper and is unraveling ever-faster behind you, taking your parents with it. "In the dream, I am given a monkey heart," writes poet Katherine Larson, "and [am] told to be careful how I love / because of the resulting infection." Maybe we each need several hearts in order to have spares, just in case. Although I live in the desert during the week, I come into the city to give poetry readings, go to the symphony, or bird the LA River, and with each transect, it's as if my memories reshuffle the deck, laying down a new face card each time. What piece of my childhood will call out next? From the Hollywood Freeway, heading into downtown, I can see my old church, and beside it, the same fan palm trees I grew up with. They are old and dear friends by now, taller but still enduring, and each time I pass, I wave at them. "Hi, guys! Hang in there. See you next time!"

Some days I am pretty sure that little shimmer and glow means they are waving back.

# Things You Can Do with Water

Los Angeles has two seasons, burning and flooding, just as Los Angeles has only two occupations, movie star and not–movie star. Freeways have two speeds, full speed and dead stop, and the land-scape, broadly speaking, has two manifestations, vertical and flat.

The steep parts are very steep, covered by manzanita, toyon, coyote brush, and poison oak in such a dense wall that biologists use two categories, hard chaparral and soft chaparral. Soft denotes pliable stems and walkable access; it is coastal and rare. Hard refers to all the rest—to scrub oaks and cactus and shrubs protected by dense wood and stiff leaves ("sclerophyllous"). Hard also describes the human experience, since bushwhacking through mature chaparral—"I'll just climb up that ridge, get my bearings"—can take all morning and wear through the stoutest pair of Carhartts.

In contrast, behold the intoxicating flat stretches between the ridges, the coastal plains that allow the map's contour lines to relax and stretch out, a landscape whose current form may seem stable, even inevitable, but which originally (before the nail salons and pot shops and drive-thru churches) was all a boggy, sloshy mess.

In the beginning water tried to erase Los Angeles. The first European settlement—Mission San Gabriel, founded in 1771— was built too close to Whittier Narrows. It was wiped out by a flood, and the Spanish had to pack up and try again an hour's walk inland. The new mission used the same name and also the same formula: find water, steal water, hold mass, enslave los indios, call it good. By the 1780s a pueblo began to accrete near where City Hall is now, a Spaghetti Western hamlet serviced by Zanja Madre, the mother ditch, a spade-dug sluice that connected the Los Angeles River to the adobe huddle, pretending it might someday matter.

November 5, 1913: William Mulholland's aqueduct finally opened, freeing the city from the mother ditch while fleecing Owens Valley ranchers of their water rights. Before we think too long or too sadly about the bamboozled farmers of Lone Pine and Independence, it should be noted that they themselves had gotten water rights only a few years previously by driving out and/or killing and/or starving the indigenous Paiute people. On average, blood diamonds are less tainted than a glass of water from a Los Angeles faucet.

By "Los Angeles," I mean what everyone does, which is not the legal city but the combined twinklefest stretching continuously from Disneyland to Magic Mountain. At the bottom end, the sprawl of greater LA nearly reaches San Diego; on the north, Los Angeles stops once I-5 grinds its slow way up past Piru, Castaic, and Pyramid Lakes. Once you get to the brake check pullouts and runaway truck ramps, you are no longer in Los Angeles, you are in the mountains, and for now—just this once—the mountains do not concern us.

Hard to envision, but until the 1800s coastal Los Angeles was a dynamic landscape, shimmering with mirage, reshaping itself with each storm, offering pockets of shade and cool water even on the hottest summer days. T.S. Eliot said that a river is a brown god. That is true, at least here. Historically, until very recently, much of the coastal plain was seasonally flooded, as the major river systems—the Los Angeles, San Gabriel, and Santa Ana Rivers, each flowing from the mountains to the sea—slithered back and forth like fire hoses on a polished gym floor. Deltas formed and dissolved; floods filled the low places between ridges with standing water many feet deep. Some years the rivers and marshes and the once-dry, now-submerged parts all connected, and Los Angeles and Orange Counties turned into a single, continuous lake.

Before I moved to the desert I used to live at the beach, so each week to see my parents I drove up and down the 605 freeway from sea level to the foothills. The 605 freeway parallels—and on maps, is named after—the San Gabriel River, which is often out of view, hidden in its bed like a recalcitrant convict sent to the hole. Driving, you are above everything: the houses, the riverbed, even nature itself. It's almost as if we think we're now post-water. And yet driving, especially in Los Angeles, we ride on the bones of water. Whether you are building a freeway or a parking garage or the Rose Bowl Stadium, to make something out of concrete you need a slurry of cement and aggregate, which is poured over (or sprayed onto) a lattice of rebar. Aggregate—a mix of sand and rocks—is basically grated mountainside that flashfloods have sent crashing down the canyons. The debris spreads out in alluvial fans. Move ahead to now, and when we want concrete, quarries are built at the mouths of canyons to mine the outwash, sort it, and deliver it in trucks to construction sites. All freeways were built not just on top of water, but from the history of water.

Not so long ago, before car lots, and before the beet fields and dairy farms that the car lots displaced, the San Gabriel River was only one wetter, deeper part of a network of interconnected habitats. We could itemize these multiple marshland components—vernal pools, brackish sloughs, feeder creeks, alkali meadows, willow forests—but the list of different habitats would run past twenty entries. Let botanists worry about the distinctions: what matters is not how many ways an ecologist can subdivide a swamp, but the sheer variety of swampiness overall. The flatland of pre-settlement California was an encyclopedia of wetness.

Place names along the 605 eulogize forgotten habitats. Santa Fe Springs was the site of healing waters, "Holy Faith Springs." The city of Lakewood—that postwar tract land so vividly memorialized by D.J. Waldie—had such saturated aquifers that it was once the site of an artesian well gone rogue. An 1895 wildcat strike was a real gusher: the blown well sported a plume of water 80 feet high, sustained by a flow of 2,300 gallons a minute. The runoff accumulated in a pond that covered two hundred acres. The town of Los Alamitos means "little cottonwoods"; cottonwood trees require river corridors to thrive, especially when the trees are young. *Aliso*, a word repeated in the names of towns, apartments, schools, and gas storage fields, is Spanish for alder, another *agua*-centric tree.

If traffic locked up on the 605, then I took the 405 to visit Mom and Dad. First I would pass the Goodyear Blimp's mooring site and defense industry plants and LAX, then head up the grade towards UCLA. This was once all water too. Nathan Masters reminds us that a "complex of meadows, ponds, marshes, and pools stretched from Mid-City Los Angeles to South L.A." The major north-south street called La Cienega translates as "the marsh," borrowed from the Spanish land grant of the same name. Masters: "In present-day Beverly Hills, a network of streams flowed from the Hollywood Hills into a large area dominated by sedges and rushes. Part of the Spanish name for these meadows—*Rodeo de las Aguas*, or Round-Up of the Waters—lives on in the name of Rodeo Drive." We remember the origin even in pronunciation, since everybody says the name of the shopping district the three-syllable Spanish way: *roe-DAY-oh* (instead of *ROAD-ee-oh*, the cowboy event).

When I was young, I lived on the Atwater side of the Los Angeles River but had friends on the other bank too, in Frogtown and Silver Lake, and my mother worked at Logan Elementary School in Echo Park, west over a low set of hills. With a bike I explored like an unleashed Davey Crockett, expanding the radius on each trip. I wasn't even sure where I was sometimes—Echo Park, what's that? Now gentrified and arty, Echo Park used to be mostly blue collar and immigrant, with the occasional quirky musician or kinky sex shop. It was in Echo Park that Aimee Semple McPherson, faith healer and charismatic saver of ten thousand souls at a time, built Angelus Temple in 1923, creating the first megachurch in California. Her name has faded from cultural memory but the church is still there, overlooking the thirty-acre lake and park.

What we now call Echo Park Lake began as Reservoir

No. 4, when excavations in the 1860s expanded a stream into an impoundment intended to hold drinking water siphoned out of the Los Angeles River. By the 1890s No. 4 had evolved into a decorative lake and the Keystone Kops were banned from filming there because they trampled the flowers. Photographs from the 1920s reveal a tree-lined water feature as calm and benign as a lagoon on the Amalfi Coast. I loved this park when I discovered it in the 1960s. If I had an afternoon off from helping my mom at her school, I would walk over and scatter bread for the ducks. Technically it is not a lake, it is a detention basin for storm runoff. Whatever the name, by the 1990s the water had become eutrophic and the park had become a bit dodgy, even by LA standards. A reset button was pushed, and after dredging and a makeover, Echo Park Lake once more offers a geyser-tall fountain, pedal-powered swan boats, lotus flowers and canary palms and fan palms; and provides a shoreline for local kids trying to feed pigeons uncooked rice to see if it will expand in their stomachs and make the birds explode. Visiting now I notice things I overlooked as a child. I especially like the boathouse with its Mission Revival lighthouse—Padre Serra meets Cape Cod.

Water is power, metaphorically but also literally. Among other odd ideas, in the 1880s Echo Park Lake was intended to provide power to textile mills, in an attempt to turn Los Angeles into Lowell, Massachusetts, the poster child for the Industrial

Revolution. Being adjacent to the Merrimack and Concord Rivers gave the factories of Lowell access to free energy, and being close to Boston Harbor, the mills could import cotton from the South and export finished cloth to Europe. Los Angeles did not have any of those things and the mill idea was utterly daft. Still, common sense never got in the way before, and the conduit did flow briefly.

In the end, what came to be known as Woolen Mill Ditch only powered one small mill. When that failed, an ice factory was built on the site, which also failed. Finally, the project was abandoned. The central tenet of the American Dream may be to get other schmucks to invest in your dream just long enough for you to cash out and go someplace else.

A mix of creek freaks and ecological historians, studying archival maps and the distribution patterns of sycamores, groundtruthing their hunches, have figured out where at least some of the pre-pavement water used to flow. The streams may be filled in and paved over, but we can honor their ghost sites anyway. I have followed similar investigations, albeit less systematically. For me, as a dumb kid just messing around on rainy days, I had no idea that maps could tell me what I wanted to know, which was where did all this water come from and where was it going? *Of course* Los Angeles was connected to Atlantis—you could see it so plainly. Presto chango: with enough rain, even a modest hillside would reveal forgotten waterfalls. I had a morbid fixation with following the flows to a final endpoint, and after a few blocks or a few miles I would watch muddy water churgle through iron grates to disappear into the caverns and mysteries of underground Los Angeles. Squatting down in the gutter, wet past the knees, I wondered who or what lived down there, and if I got sucked in, would there be any way out?

The water is still here, and it is still coming. We talk about hundred-year storms, but what about a thousand-year storm or a five-thousand-year storm? We might have five-thousand-year storms every two hundred fifty years—we have no way of being sure. The weather event does not even have to be exceptional. Meteorologists call a certain category of storms the Pineapple Express. This is a big, wet, midwinter storm that drenches not just the mountains and lowlands but melts the snowpack, too. These storms hit hard and can last for days; another term is "atmospheric river." Even just five or six pineapple doozies in a row and we will see changes few people are prepared for. If flood-water overtops the banks of the Los Angeles River, the "oops-we-built-the-tract-below-grade-level" shock will happen at the same time that entire towns disappear under an ocean of muddy water. If residents are lucky, their roofs will stick out, making each house an island with a marooned and desperate family waving at the rescue helicopters—assuming the helicopter bases don't flood as well, nor the freeways the pilots need to traverse before reporting for duty.

According to the *Los Angeles Times*, if the LA or San Gabriel Rivers overtop their banks, that would turn "sections of Long Beach, Carson, Lakewood, Compton, Downey, and West Covina into flood zones. Coastal flooding could inundate areas such as Belmont Shore, Naples, and Seal Beach, and the ports of Los Angeles and Long Beach." Things we can do with water: watch $800 billion in property damage happen in twenty minutes, and nobody will be able to do a blessed thing to stop it.

One of the early Spanish names for Los Angeles was *El Pueblo de Nuestra Señora la Reina de los Ángeles sobre el Río Porciúncula*, or "the Town of Our Lady the Queen of the Angels next to the River associated with St. Francis of Assisi." We can do better than that, surely. Why not just "Our Lady of the River"? *Nuestra Señora del Río*—or perhaps our lady of the deep, magical, still-flowing river, the home-of-steelhead-and-carp river, the toxic river, the bitter river, the patient river, the starlit river.

There was a tanker spill once; jet fuel ran through the culverts: the orange-with-fire river. The river of helicopters and tagging, car chases and sad poets. Because for me, at least, the Los Angeles River is a good place to go to think. It's where I saw a mastiff bat—largest bat in North America—while on a long, mid-December bike ride from Burbank past the Glendale Narrows and on to Downtown. Things had been going badly and I was deep into the blues. Then I saw it. A bat? In winter? Yes, since it was still warm enough for midge swarms. Saw it, stopped, got off the bike, had a drink of water, took out my journal, and began to write. First time in weeks I had written something joyful instead of recycling the usual fears and resentments.

Tarot card river: you've just inverted the Hanged Man.

River of hope and litigation.

Ten expensive new bridges: *Architectural Digest* river. The *vato* and drive-by river, the addicted river, the hard-sided river of bloodstain and rebar. River of yellow angel's trumpet (poisonous), water hemlock (poisonous), oleander (poisonous), castor bean (poisonous). The river of cochineal and scabs.

The merciful river.

The grizzly river and the rattlesnake river.

And always, just out of sight, the biding-its-time river.

We may ignore water, take it for granted, think we have run out of things to do with it. Yet someday in America our rivers will remember where they came from, where they used to go, what things they still know how to do. Water will come again. When it does, slabs of concrete the size of garage doors will peel off and raft away, and the brown gods of water will wave and roar in unison.

Things we can do with water: look at it nervously, hoping it will stay in one place.

Things water can do with us: wipe it all clean and ask us to start again.

# Divorce Insurance

The last person to escape from the burning *Hindenburg* was a professional acrobat, which just goes to show we never can tell how our odd career choices may save our lives later. I am sure somebody in his life had once said, "Acrobat? *Really*? Why not banking—something steady, more reliable?"

In high school I thought I was going to work trail crews for a living but ended up going to college, and once there, ended up as an English major because it turned out that as an English major I could get an A on a paper and not do the homework first. Since I was generally working two jobs and commuting by bicycle, I needed all the tailwind God was willing to spare. I had also tried history as a major, then geography—late in college I came across art history, but by then it was too late to switch. I liked literature well enough and could crank out papers quickly, so there we go. Life path? Not so much "find your passion" as a case of "try not to get lost in the fog."

Sometimes I dropped out of college and worked in a factory or washed dishes, but obviously that sucked, so back to Dickinson I went, back to Blake and Wilfred Owen and Siegfried Sassoon. I did like Coleridge—"This Lime-Tree Bower My Prison," the one where everybody goes for a walk and he stays home because he has a bum leg. In the end he writes a better account of the hike than if he had gone in person. That seems like a good way to do the PCT: sit at home with a burned leg resting on a pillow and imagine your trip all the way bottom to top, Mexico to Canada, and be sure to imagine some rain and a cold wind and being out of food one day and trading a fresh pack of Moleskin tape for somebody's last Pop-Tart.

Funded by a grant, I spent one summer in Moab, rock climbing and writing a book about John Wesley Powell, the one-armed Civil War veteran and Colorado River explorer. My total monthly budget was $300, but luckily for me, Moab had hit the slack water between uranium and the still-to-come mountain bike boom; there were free places to camp and nobody else had any money either. I was still trying to decide on a direction for my life. On rest days, if I ran into one of the rangers at the coin-op or the market, I would ask how they had come into that line of work.

One Ed Abbey look-alike was a math teacher who mainly needed a summer paycheck, while a deeply tanned brother and sister had come to the Park Service through a shared love of geology, which had started as children on vacations in the Southwest. One tall, gaunt fellow—"Just call me Slim, as in, 'your chances are slim to none'"—explained to me that he had been in Vietnam, and when asked on his application about search and rescue experience, had ticked the box "yes," on the notion that search-and-destroy was close enough for government work.

My favorite answer was given by a ranger named Rebecca. She was staffing the entrance station at Arches. With no other cars behind me, she leaned out the window to talk, and I turned off the engine.

For her, a nature job was a kind of divorce insurance—not income, but medicine. "Look," she explained, "if you knew you might be sick a lot, you would make sure to live near a hospital or at least a good pharmacy. For me, sooner or later I am going to have a bad day, a bad month, maybe even a bad year."

Yes, sure, I agreed. We all go through a low period when, as Melville says, the hypos get the better of us.

"So, given what any of us will go through," she said, "and given that nature does heal, then it makes sense to get a job where you have regular access to nature, either during the job itself or on days off."

We both had to agree that in an equation like that, what you need to survive is ready at hand, in infinite supply. "Who knows," she said, handing me back my access pass. "It might be such good juju, it will keep the bad stuff away in the first place."

I thought of that years later when my turn for the mopes and the blues came up. It was indeed a divorce, or a separation from a marriage that maybe still could be saved, we were not quite sure. In any case, I ended up living alone in a house with no furniture but a good view. The furniture part was easy: in the empty dining room I installed a ping-pong table, and on a thrift store end table next to it, I set out a silver, star-shaped basket filled with bright orange ping-pong balls. Who cared if some got lost in the light fixtures or decorated all the top window ledges just out of reach? More where those came from. *Whack*—that ping-pong table and the basin of endless balls made me popular with local children and tipsy but enthusiastic fellow teachers.

Most birders keep lists of birds seen from their yards, and in my new solitude I decided to get good at scoping mine— scanning all the time from the kitchen window, binoculars ready on the counter. Sometimes I just took a chair into the yard and waited to see a rising kettle of northbound pelicans, or to hear the *kee-eer, kee-eer* of a pair of red-shouldered hawks. My spotting scope extended my vision's reach. From that house I could see a cemetery and some desert and out across the entire Antelope Valley, and on clearest days, all the way north to the start of the Sierra. One afternoon, coming back from a meeting I picked up a distant golden eagle and drove like hell (and even ran a red light) to make it to my house in time to catch it floating away over the horizon. It took every inch of reach from my Zeiss to make it out, but hey, I *did* see it—tick, another new one for the house list. No time to feel sorry for myself at night either; nights were for owls (great horned and barn).

Roadrunner, sage sparrow, thrasher: they added up, day after day, week after week. Northern flicker. Merlin. Mountain bluebird. It was like a portfolio that only got fuller—with every month of the year something migrating or readjusting or looking for a better deal one ridge over; no market corrections.

My best yard bird was not a bird but an animal. Awake one night, feeling strangely calm yet unable to sleep, I went through the dark house looking out each window in turn. Something made me check the urban side, the side that faced not the desert but the houses across the way. There in the moonlight, calm and stately and in no hurry whatsoever, a bobcat was walking right down the middle of my street. One end of my cul-de-sac abutted undeveloped desert, so it made logical sense for one to be there, but in all my months of local hiking, I hadn't even seen bobcat scat, let alone the beast itself.

It made logical sense and ecological sense, but more importantly, it made *spiritual* sense. Man is a meaning-making animal, and I knew perfectly well what that bobcat was telling me. Even in Palmdale, life is indeed enchanted, and no matter how low I might feel, some little surprise, some little gift, was going to tap on my door and give me a double shot of hope and joy. It seemed like a fair divorce swap: you get to keep the love seat and the coffee maker, and I get to keep the bobcats.

The poets I studied in college, the so-called War Poets who wrote from the desolate trenches of the War to End All Wars, the Great War, the long horror show that we now call World War I, those writers had a deep appreciation for skylarks. This bird is all over British poetry, from Wordsworth's "ethereal minister" to Shelley's "blithe spirit." It's even hidden among Ted Hughes's crows. In actual fact, the skylark is a streaky finch not all that different from any other little brown job. If you saw one scratching around the weeds, it would not catch your eye—just another sparrow, boring and invisible. But if you're living in the mud and terror of a wet trench, and if your view of nature is whatever slit of sky you can make out past the parapets, then a bird with a magic voice and the lively habit of going straight up to sing from on-high—skylarking, to use the correct verb—is going to seem like a vision sent by angels. *Of course* you're going to write about it.

Let the divorces come. Illness, even cancer—yes, life is life and death is life and we all know that one way or another, endings will come. My cars will break down, my body will ache and creak, my friends will betray me. My parents will grow old, need care, at times be unpleasant, and I will probably be unpleasant right back. Sometimes I wonder if that is my family's secret motto: *If in doubt, be unpleasant.* But bless the skylarks and bless them well: even in the worst horror and wreckage of my life, there they will be, soaring up and singing, and unless I am a greater fool than I ever have been before, there I will be too, huddled in the mud, squinting to make them out against the sun, looking up and smiling and (after making sure nobody is nearby) singing right back with them just as loud and glad as I can be.

# A Small, Humble Addiction

According to my Firearm Safety Certificate, my preference for 8.5 x 11 printer paper vs. A4 paper, and even my hefty table muscle (as they call too much gut in Texas): I am fully and completely an American. By default, I drive on the right, pass on the left, vote on Tuesdays, and make my veggie lasagna with eggplant, not aubergine. I take vacations, not holidays, and I agree with Roger Tory Peterson that mockingbirds whup nightingale butt, just as I agree with poet Charles Olson that the core fact of American experience is SPACE, and as he says, we write it large "because it comes larger here." For us settlers, the prairies were big, bright, and anvil hard. And after the Great Plains? Then came the Rockies, the Great Basin, the Donner Party stranded in the winter Sierra. Let's be honest: The most significant declivity in England, Cheddar Gorge, could be dropped into Bryce Canyon and vanish without scratching the furniture. (And besides, "Cheddar Gorge" sounds like what you do when you overindulge at a wine-tasting party.)

And yet—

And yet—

Do you ever wake up some mornings thinking you were born into the wrong body, the wrong life? You look around, and as Talking Heads suggests, you realize you have found yourself "in a beautiful house / With a beautiful wife / And you may ask yourself, well / How did I get here?" My predilection is for sprawling vulgarity, yet a strange and inextricable part of me wants to wear bespoke shoes and touch my Oyster Card on the pad as I run to catch a Northern Line train for High Barnet. To stay informed I will have my two regular papers, *The Guardian* and *The Sun* (the second well hidden in my briefcase), and I will step smartly into the arriving train car, never wanting to inconvenience others behind me. The prerecorded voice does not need to remind me: I already know to mind the gap.

This desire for a different me, the *real* me, this most British of possible Charles Hoods, is most present when it comes to field guides.

Ours suck; theirs do not.

Maybe that's not fair—Sibley's bird book is a fine effort, and my own field guides hold a small, warm place in my heart— but what *is* true is that we don't have nearly enough variety and quirkiness and coverage, not compared to Britain and Ireland. Unlike us, they have multiple field guides to lichen (how I burn with envy, coveting these), and eight choices when it comes to a handbook to identify mushrooms. I even own a guidebook to British roundabouts.

According to a recent email from my UK book dealer—and if my family loved me, they would stage an intervention to get me clean of NHBS, Natural History Book Service—the British moth options have grown even more plentiful. Just sticking to recent releases, one can choose between *The Atlas of Britain and Ireland's Larger Moths* and *Moths: Their Biology, Diversity and Evolution*. Want lighter fare? Try *A Concise Guide to the Moths of Great Britain and Ireland*, which would be a good supplement to *A Comprehensive Guide to Insects of Britain and Ireland*. Why get that one? Because the revised and expanded edition now has "544 pages and covers 2,300 species, with updated maps and over 2,900 color photographs." I need one of these, and right now.

In contrast, here in North America—home to such extravagant manifestations of destiny as the bison, the bighorn sheep, and the spirit bear—we don't have a field guide to mammals even half as good as what the British have for bugs. Fiona Reid wrote and painted the Peterson mammal guide, but she was limited by the mandated format of the series: she was allowed to be good but not much better than good. You can judge a nation's climb towards the apex of civilization by its mosques and cathedrals, by its on-tap IPA, but also by its ability to notice its resident Tortoiseshells and Skippers, its Brimstones and Black Rustics. In Europe generally and in the UK in particular, they have loads of books on butterflies and other insects. Here in America, our attitudes are less generous and our breadth of knowledge less comprehensive. We not only ignore nature, but too often are overtly hostile towards it. When I mentioned I was thinking about doing a book on California insects, a friend suggested a new marketing slogan. Given local prejudices, she said an appropriate subtitle might be, "Bugs: Not Just for Squishing!"

Everything about British nature books works for me: the attention to place, the exquisite details, the implied promise that if I too wander around the Lake District, I will start to write like Wordsworth or John Ruskin (or better yet, Beatrix Potter). Each day, more books arrive. How should I feel about my compulsion? "A small, humble addiction," as a shopkeeper in Cornwall once described my book fetish. Supposedly, drug dealers don't take credit cards. They should—NHBS certainly does. I hope Brexit doesn't mess up the flow, but for now, if a UK publisher doesn't produce the book I want, somebody in London can get it for me from anywhere in the world. *Bats of Estonia?* No problem: how many do you need? *Butterflies of Malaysia and Singapore?* Of course. Click here. Yesterday I was ecstatic to see that it had finally arrived, all 1,000 pages and 4.3 kilos of it: *The Handbook of the Mammals of the World, Volume 9: Bats*. It may not be the heaviest book I own, but it comes close. Abbreviated HMW, this series concludes its decades-long survey with this volume on bats, the final volume in the series, and we can expect it to be the best-illustrated, most comprehensive guidebook to bats that will exist for many years to come.

Great book, necessary book, delightful book. Not easily available in North America, though. Even Amazon does not have one in stock. It lists it as a possibility, but only with a shipping surcharge of $60 and a delivery time of three to five weeks. Not to be a crybaby, but I have to ask in frustration and envy, *Why them and not us?*

(1) They have so many field guides in England because it rains all the time there, and what else can they do except fill up notebooks and press flowers into albums? That's perhaps unkind (though it does rain a lot).

(2) It's an island so small you are never more than seventy miles from the sea. Britain, for all its history and cultural complexity, is still just a small, densely settled smudge on the world map. You can write (or study) field guides with some hope of completion because there are many fewer things to learn and draw, nature-wise, than you would find in a single old growth redwood forest on the edge of our large and newly documented continent.

The western United States has absurd abundance—more species than seems reasonable for one region to be blessed with. Think, for example, about amphibians: frogs, toads, newts, salamanders—the non-snake, non-lizard part of the herpetological spectrum. From Cornwall to John o' Groats, there are seven native amphibians in all of Great Britain.

Seven? *Seven?*

In California the official list of amphibians has a seven in it too, except our total comes closer to seventy.

(3) Another option: Even though in America we're passionate about supporting high school football and neighborhood churches—and so in that sense, we are local down to a few city blocks—we're not local in thinking about the world we actually live in.

Now we may be getting closer to a fundamental truth. In America, identity comes less from attending Harrow versus attending Eaton, or hiking Dartmoor versus exploring the Cairngorms, and more from deciding which is more "us," Target or Walmart. (Make your choice carefully: there is a small but real difference in how you're expected to dress. Only the trashiest people wear their pajamas to Target, but to Walmart? Late at night? Not a problem.)

In Britain, accent can signify social class, just as it does here, yet it also anchors the speaker to a specific location. Even an

American can hear the difference between Cornish English and Scottish English; a native of Albion will hear much finer distinctions than those. That home ground extends into micro-rivalries and finely parsed regional identities. Essex has been called the New Jersey of England, which is to say it has a reputation for being home to chav blokes and dim tarts. One British woman I know has a clique of chums, many from and still living in Essex. When I included her in a collective reference, she took umbrage. She was not an Essex girl at all, thank you very much—she comes from Hampshire, sixty miles away.

That long-standing attachment to place means there is a market for site-specific books. You can buy a field guide just to the bees of Norfolk, or how about that classic title, now out of print, *Where to Watch Birds in the East Midlands,* in case you need to pass a bank holiday weekend in Derbyshire? Here on the Pacific Rim there is no equivalent product—no magisterial, fully illustrated *Birds of Greater Sacramento,* no second edition of *Ladybugs of the East Bay Wetlands.* We do not have a ladybugs-only book at all, but Great Britain does.

Yes, sure, we can use collective databases such as iNaturalist to zoom in on a specific site, but looking up something like California's endemic *Dudleya* species on Calflora generally requires prior knowledge. You go there to log a sighting or verify a range boundary, but not to use it the way a great field guide is meant to be used: read with tea and scones on the patio as you widen your general knowledge and make plans for your next day's hike.

Unlike a database on a website, a book is real, as real as the tree it was made from, and the best books are elegant, well-designed, and a pleasure to handle and to own. Field guides promise mastery—"Hey, you can learn this, no problem, and we will help you"—and they remind us that grandeur, surprise, and wonder are all around us everywhere, even in Derbyshire, even at the much-maligned Salton Sea.

Websites don't do that. Nobody goes to Wikipedia to fall in love with the infinite beauty and pleasure of being alive in the world. Doing a last-minute school report on bats? I am sure Wikipedia has saved many a desperate tuchus. But to have it all laid out for you, plate after plate, orchid after orchid, for that we need a great artist, a David Sibley or John Muir Laws (or Keith Hansen or Jonathon Alderfer or Josie Iselin or Fiona Reid).

More so than with aged port or handmade boots, making a really great field guide may be a project measured in decades, not years. British cetacean expert Mark Carwardine has a new whale and dolphin guide out. Was it hard to work on? He admits, "Well, it dominated my life for six years. I used to lie awake at night, worrying about whether to describe something as 'blue-gray' or 'gray-blue.' I decided to go back to original sources for everything, which meant reading twelve thousand scientific papers, poring over decades of my own field notes, and studying untold numbers of photographs and video clips." To ensure accuracy, Carwardine corresponded with experts all over the world. It took three artists to do all the plates; between them, they produced more than one thousand original pieces of art. Each range map took three days to research and draw.

Sweet Jesus and the twelve apostles, I do love this book. I would never get on a Monterey boat without having my binoculars around my neck, extra Kleenex in my pocket, and a copy of Carwardine's cetacean handbook in my bag (my *waterproof* bag: mine is a signed copy, after all), published by Bloomsbury, London, though there are branches in India, Qatar, and even that provincial outpost of tumbleweed nothingness, New York. My book falls open to page 248 because I have turned to it so often: Gervais's beaked whale. Sixteen feet long, Gray above and pale below. Tropical Atlantic. Females have tiger stripes. Looks a sloe-eyed dolphin that got stuck in the taffy puller. What do you think—if I book a boat trip out of Cape Hatteras, will I see one this time? Missed them before there, but then Jon Hall went, the top mammal spotter of all, and he got one. Will it be my turn next? I check under "behavior" and read the three most common words in beaked whale biology: "virtually nothing known."

In the end, if I am honest with myself, I value British field guides not just because I want to be better informed when I travel abroad, and not just because bird names like *corn crake* please the shit out of me, and certainly not to support the British publishing industry, long may it wave. Those are valid points of contact, but more importantly, I buy and own and read (and treasure and hoard) British field guides because I love discovering all over again that the ordinary, everyday world is known and valued with such exquisite devotion.

Faith and science make better dance partners than popular culture usually admits. Both believe that the past informs the future and both center on the close reading of a text—what is a spiderweb if not a site of infinite mystery? From psalters to bestiaries, animals have embodied stories and ideas. It is easy to agree with the claim that field guides began with illuminated manuscripts. You are reading the book of Matthew when out trundles a perfectly rendered hedgehog or dung beetle, or else the margins flash purple with a sudden swirl of pansies, aka heartsease ("heart's ease"). The Getty Museum owns a manuscript from 1590 that has a dragonfly so precisely drawn it could appear in a book today. As an experiment, I downloaded a high-res version and opened it on my sharpest photo-editing monitor. Sure enough, I could identify it to species: *Brachytron pratense* or hairy hawker—"among the first dragonflies to emerge in spring."

It is tempting to see in daily news reports proof of our worst selves—humans are vicious and genocidal, and a general pox upon the natural world. Yet with a great field guide, we have a chance to become intimate with the best side of human nature. A good book reminds us how many people have the capacity to be attentive, loving, artistic, and, in the end, even able to tell a Belted Beauty from a Barberry Carpet.

Both moth species are scribbled with brown and black. A similar kind, the Rannoch Brindled Beauty, is brown the same way, but sports a narrow band of orange dots. Its habitat preference? "Boggy acid moorland and dry heathland."

Easy to tell the three species apart...*I think.*

I had better order one more book, just to make sure.

# Confessions
# of
# an
# Amateur

Look, I am sorry, but when it comes to pine trees, I still can't tell a ponderosa pine from a Jeffrey pine.

I should be able to—I own eight tree books, after all—but I remain unsure. Both trees are tall, straight, timber-grade conifers of the American West with puzzle-piece bark whose fissures smell like vanilla. Unless it is only the bark of the Jeffrey pine that smells like vanilla, not the ponderosa, though I have stood next to people who swear a given ponderosa smells so much like vanilla it makes them jones bad for pecan pie and oatmeal cookies. One of the two species smells like vanilla, anyway, unless it's not so much vanilla as butterscotch, or is it more like pineapple schnapps? And maybe both kinds smell like that?

There has to be some feature to tell the pines apart, professionally and with confidence. The cones—the cones of one have knurled barbs, while those of the other don't? When first discovered in 1852 near Mt. Shasta, the Jeffrey pine was assumed to be a subspecies of ponderosa. Experts struggle, even today.

If you wanted to know the closest Jeffrey pine to you right now, you could find out on iNaturalist, that compendium of citizen-science data whose digital filing cabinets expand daily. I recently uploaded three snake records and a vermillion flycatcher from a park in Palmdale, but I don't often post to iNaturalist, nor to sister site eBird. And since I birdwatch but don't regularly post my day lists, my passage through nature leaves no wake. I am not contributing to the common good, which means in some way I am still just an amateur.

I don't submit daily birding tallies for several related reasons. The first has to do with managing anxiety, competition, my need to complete a full set. I know my faults, and if I have submitted nine eBird checklists in a row, one every day for a week and two days, I know what happens next. I will want to submit something the tenth day as well, and will be cross if the quotidian obligations of daily life cut me off from posting a strong "Day 10" list. I might even want that list to be the best one yet: out of all the ten-in-a-row lists, let me make sure the final one has the most species overall plus one or two cracking good rarities...and there go all my daylight hours.

When did nature become such hard work?

What about just saying, "I don't know what kind of tree it

was—but it sure smelled nice"? The data fields don't have a category like that.

When it comes to nature, we are encouraged to nail down specificity: we want to know what everything is, and know *right now*. I am guilty of feeding the beast as much as anybody else. As a small-time nature expert, I have spouted off on local TV, on the radio, in the newspaper, in podcasts and blogs, and along the way, I have been asked some daffy questions, some impossible-to-answer-honestly-on-air questions, and some questions that somebody knows the answer to, just not me. That last category includes this: "How many species of insects are there in California?" (I answered "ten thousand," which is just this side of a wild guess.)

What if there's nothing to say, or, equally likely, what if the expert is just a quasiexpert—knowledgeable about something, just not the topic at hand? "Flash—this just in—something moderately atypical has happened, and nobody knows what the heck it means."

Being amateur is the normal state of most people most of the time, so it deserves higher status than it usually gets. It is a deeply liberating state to inhabit. I *like* not knowing all the answers. As the UK birder Simon Barnes says, even an expert birder is an amateur the minute he flies to a new country. That is why I love being a crap butterfly watcher. I might not know the names of half the species I am looking at, but so what. I love making up my own nonce names to fill the void, while trying to guess which zag it is going to zig next. (Butterflies do seem to have a bad case of, "Oh wait, what was I just doing?") Watching them, I am completely unbothered by the fact that I can't tell if the butterfly in question is feeding, mating, celebrating the summer solstice, or just searching for a quiet bush on which to perch and die. To me, butterflies are about color, movement, pleasure, and surprise. The science is irrelevant.

Amateurs don't know things can't be done. One of the great things about Charles Darwin going around the world on the *Beagle* is that he was a raving amateur the whole time. As the joke goes, if he were alive today, he couldn't get into grad school—his grades were too bad. He skipped more lectures than he attended, although he did sit in on a talk by one famous visitor, the American rustic John James Audubon.

What to do with somebody with such tenuous professional prospects? Darwin's grandparents, founders of Wedgwood china, put him on a boat as Captain Fitzroy's companion, hoping it would help errant Charles get his act together and manage to become somebody of merit, a "somebody" like Grandpa Erasmus, the famous poet. So there Darwin was, a wealthy dilettante, finding marine fossils in the Andes and witnessing a tsunami in Chile, not knowing he was supposed to have gotten a degree in geology first.

I assume if I were really dialed into the right way to be a butterfly watcher, I would covet a different pair of binoculars, or would know that it is too late or too early in the season to see whatever I'm hoping to see. Not knowing that it's the wrong time of year, I go out anyway. Lucky me: too ignorant to know that I probably won't have a grand time. Today I see the Mimosa, the Greater and Lesser Brass Knuckles, and the Mummy's Cravat. Oh, those are not the right names? They are now; here they are in my journal. Yesterday was even better, when I saw a strong flight of Skull-Spotted Bonnet Snatchers, attracted to their favorite bush, the Flaming Snot-Knob.

Charlie Chaplin once said that all humans are amateurs, since we're not around long enough to get really good at being people. That might be especially true if you compare us to trees: the oldest ponderosa pine we know about is in Utah, and it is 943 years old. Ponderosa pine was first brought into formal science by David Douglas, a Scotsman who is remembered in the name for the Douglas fir. He died in Hawai'i when he fell into a trap set for feral cattle, unless he was murdered by a cattle hunter for the contents of his wallet. John Jeffrey also was Scottish; after several years in the Pacific Northwest, he was last seen in San Francisco (some accounts say San Diego), planning to cross the California desert. So far as we know, he died alone, but if he passed away near trail companions, in my perfect world they would have built his coffin entirely from planks of freshly milled Jeffrey pine.

I once had a small cluster of oak trees named after me in San Joaquin Marsh, on the university side of the road across from the water treatment plant. I am no forester, but I helped plant them, water them, protect them from development. Hood Grove, the trees are called. Note to my kids: when the time comes, if you wanted to build my coffin from scratch, one of those trees might be an appropriate donor. I know you've never made a coffin before, so just scribble dimensions on scratch paper and follow your heart.

It doesn't have to be elegant. My Skilsaw is in a milk crate under the workbench; the extension cords are by the kibble bin.

Don't forget to turn out the lights when you're done.

# Today
# I Will
# Draw
# a Penguin

Penguin meat tastes like rancid beef marinated in cod liver oil, which is to say it tastes better than starving to death, or so we learn from the journals of Antarctic explorers. Even better (at least from the explorers' perspective), if there is one penguin, there will be a thousand, so pass the salt.

The word *penguin* is older than Shakespeare and like the word *whisky*, probably entered English from Gaelic. The term used to apply to the great auk, now clobbered into extinction for its meat and eggs, then got transferred south. Contemporary zoos know to pander to popular taste and so they feature penguins ahead of ugly animals (bush pigs) and boring animals (most small cats nap all day). They're not as good as pandas, but pretty high up there. The San Diego Zoo has a new penguin display with a glass-fronted tank that holds two hundred thousand gallons of water, thirteen feet deep. That sounds modern and luxe, but does anybody besides me remember going to the San Diego Zoo back when the tour bus drivers would spin slices of bread into the bear pits as they passed? The bears were paunchy but nimble; they caught every piece. Before it moved to a new site with new policies, the old LA Zoo allowed visitors to feed the elephants. The eager pachyderms would stretch their trunks through the bars and pluck peanuts out of your open hand, shell and all.

This is animal husbandry from the dark ages—stories from the bad old days when moms smoked Newport Menthols and cars didn't come with seatbelts, or if they did, nobody made you wear them. If you want a real blast from the past, check out *Mutual of Omaha's Wild Kingdom*. Marlin Perkins and sidekick Jim Fowler deliver stilted dialogue and faux conservation wisdom, periodically pausing to wrestle captive animals passed off as wild ones— or rather, Jim does the wrasslin', while Marlin watches from the safety of the jeep.

Zoos today trade animals among themselves, hoping for genetic diversity and trying to keep populations balanced—one place has too many gazelles and not enough elands, and so they arrange a swap. Yet beneath that, zoos rest on a legacy of capture we rarely think about. Every lion, tiger, polar bear, ostrich, wallaby, and python in the zoo today came from an ancestor captured in the wild, put in a crate, and stevedored up the gangplank to be taken back to the mother country. It's what we do, we humans. If we see a plant we like, we grab it and stick it in the ground someplace else. Pretty bird? Cage it in the kitchen, listen to it sing. Partly it's a misplaced desire to be closer to nature, and partly it's because ownership demonstrates status, whether you're a cartel boss having a hippopotamus delivered to your jungle estate, or you're William Randolph Hearst, whose zebra herd still grazes the San Simeon grasslands. We're good at moving things around, but not so hot at putting them back when we're done.

Bread-fed bears are not good enough anymore, which is why any aquarium or zoo worth its salted mackerel needs to have a top-notch penguin display. Common species in captivity include Magellanic and Humboldt penguins from South America, and their twin, the African penguin, formerly called jackass penguin after its braying call. Don't get too *aww, how cute.* According to *Birds of the World,* "penguins are tough, dense, efficient deepwater predators, much more likely to bite you (hard!) or whack you with a flipper than cuddle or shake your hand." Still, we do like them—we like them very much. Point and gawk: the first still-alive, non-stuffed penguin arrived in London in 1865—a king penguin taken in the Falkland Islands. It was followed by a rockhopper (1873), gentoo (1874), African (1882), blue (1887), and yellow-crested (1891).

What was the mortality rate on the voyage north? Hard to get an honest count, but some sources imply 90 percent of the cargo didn't make it. The return on investment of populating zoos is something I have puzzled over many times. In order to work on a book about polar aviation I went to Antarctica twice, once staying with the Chileans on King George Island and once as an artist-in-residence when I was assigned to the US bases at McMurdo Station and the South Pole. On these trips of course I saw (and photographed and drew) penguins, including the lister's holy grail, the emperor penguin. How many layers of reality does it take to build the truth? When I was interviewing pilots for my book, sometimes my sources would look around, drop their voices, and ask if I wanted to know "the *real* story about penguins." But of course, old sport—here, let me turn to a new page in my journal.

One piece of aviation lore I heard is this: I can't verify it, but supposedly just before they rotated home to the States, American helicopter pilots would feign mechanical trouble, set down on the ice, grab two or three penguins, shove them in a sack, gun it back to base, walk in late to debriefing, and throw up their hands, "Who, me?"

*Something hinky in the fuel line so's I had to touch down out on the ice, but don't worry, I got that booger hosed out clean.*

Meanwhile a buddy sticks the contraband in a tank, tosses in a fistful of anchovies, seals it up. Grease pencil marks the lid SCIENCE, DO NOT OPEN. Pilots take the crate with them on their flights back home—urgent science coming through, priority transfer at each station. Navy guys, they don't make that much money, and it's not like there's not a whole lot more penguins where those came from.

Did that really happen? Some swear yes and some just as quickly say no. Count it as hearsay, but supposedly the San Francisco Zoo filled an entire penguin grotto that way.

True or not, we do know that attitudes about zoos—what to put in them, and how zoo staff should behave—have changed since then. A newspaper photograph from 1949 shows four Humboldt penguins being released into their new pen at the LA Zoo. There are two keepers, both white, both male. They have on khaki uniforms that soldiers in World War II called suntans.

In what looks to be harsher than it might actually have been, one keeper shoos the penguins with a piece of plywood while the other prods them with a stick. The plywood keeper wears a pith helmet and is smoking a pipe while he works; stick prodder has on a white Jughead beanie. It was not supposed to be an unkind photo; probably it was intended to provide some human interest on a slow news day. Catalog notes document the fact that the zookeepers had named the four penguins Mo, Smo, Andy, and Mandy. What the penguins named the keepers, we do not know.

Since penguins in captivity can live thirty years, I may have seen Mo myself. Toting a bag of colored pencils and a pad of newsprint, I used to ride my bike to the LA Zoo, hoping to draw lions and bears. If those were asleep, I would make do by sketching the flamingos. If I wanted a break, I went to the easy things like hippos and especially penguins, since they are basically bowling pins in dinner jackets. Those were good days, special days, days I have tried to recreate standing in front of penguin colonies in Cape Town and Tierra del Fuego. I should know better than to spend too much time on Nostalgia Island, though—it costs too much, for one thing. (I recently met a boomer spending $100,000 to restore a '68 Camaro, the car he could not afford in high school.) Perhaps I should rely on the folk wisdom of riddles for guidance. "What is black and white and red all over?" Of the possible choices—a well-read newspaper, a road-killed skunk, an embarrassed zebra—maybe the best one has been there all along: penguins, penguins, and the thin red line that runs from dreams to responsibilities, from the past to now, the line that runs from me to the rest of the beating hearts on this strange, penguin-blessed planet.

# Love and Sex in Natural History Dioramas

## *here come the bears*

Most people coming to Alaska want to see bears, and Ted Stevens Airport in Anchorage obliges. It can't show live bears—it is, sorry to report, an airport, not a zoo—so it offers a selection of stuffed bears in glass cases. Many people seem to enjoy taking pictures of them or with them, since a big, tall, fierce bear marks frontier-ness in a visually compelling way. And the airport doesn't just have half a dozen bears, but also has a stuffed moose, a musk ox, a leaping deer, a pair of tundra swans, and the world's largest halibut. The airport is part transit hub, part natural history museum. "Welcome to Alaska," the airport seems to say. "Let's all go out and kill things."

### sorry to state the obvious, but—

Taxidermy begins only after an animal dies. Airport displays and museum dioramas rely on a postmortem art that needs to recycle some or all of a once-living, now-deceased organism. To love nature this way, to admire its beauty and power, we first need somebody to kill nature, peel off its skin, create a plaster or latex mold, and build it fresh, faithful to the last whisker. And yet it works: when done well, taxidermy works. Upright, polar bears stand eleven feet tall. To most of us, that is just a number. Hard to internalize that, to understand that it's not an animal, it is some kind of immense tree, a tree with teeth and claws, a white bear tree that weighs more than your car. I have seen real polar bears, alive and in the wild, and I have seen zoo polar bears, fur greened by algae, and each encounter was moving in its own way. Each encounter was also from a distance. Zoos have fences and moats; in Svalbard, you're on a boat when you see most polar bears, or, if hiking, you are guarded by an armed guide. To get a better sense of how freaking huge this species truly is, go to the airport in Alaska and stand under one, looking up. Then you will know.

### particle physics part 1

But how can I enjoy seeing a stuffed bear? It is dead. A human killed it and put it on display. Given the choice, wouldn't most of us wish the animal could have lived out the rest of its life in some kind of natural span, rather than suddenly receive a round (or who knows, maybe six rounds) of .375 Holland & Holland magnum? I look at a stuffed bear then turn away quickly, wincing and troubled. In Anchorage or anywhere, it is not right to like—and tolerate—needless death. I feel that same attraction-revulsion when I think about animal dioramas in natural history museums (hereafter, NHMs). As theatrical space, a row of lit-from-within nature dioramas in a grand, dark hall is sexy and inimitable. There is a churchy element, and it's a little like doing the stations of the cross, but you can go in any order and the imperative is to learn, not repent. A good diorama constructs a clear narrative and shrink-rays a hypothetical moment in time, stopping the clock at one specific moment. This frozen-in-time aspect promises, *This is what this kind of nature looked like on this exact day.* We have stepped out of our time machines at just the exact right instant, and the scene tells a story about what lives where and who eats whom; it also lets us know who in the family is the mommy, the daddy, the baby. The scene is always prelapsarian; contrails never cross the sky, and if there is a cliff full of squabbling kittiwakes, there is never a window that takes us to that most coveted of gull feeding grounds, the active landfill. Some of the diorama's inhabitants may have entered into the museum's collection as roadkill, but roadkill itself makes no appearance, in part because there are no roads—and also no trails, benches, cairns, port-a-potties, or trash bins. It is nature and yet not nature, and the artistry of presentation makes it easy to ignore the fact that we are looking at very dead, very manipulated animals. These are not even average or typical animals, which in the real world can be runty or dinged up or missing an ear. Each of these animals is a prime choice select, the perfect embodiment of size and symmetry. Bowing to visitors' patriarchal expectations, the male animal takes his centerpiece role as protector of females and lesser creatures. (We can tell he is the dad: he has the biggest horns and likes to drive.) When I see animal dioramas, I feel bad and good at the same time, inhabiting the same flickering moment of singularity as light does when it is both a particle and a wave. Quantum mechanics thus allows for an endless indeterminacy, and that is how dioramas work for me. They are useful, attractive, artistic, but also colonial and limiting and laden with daddy issues. I love them, but that love rides in a chariot pulled by the twin dogs of shame and doubt.

## the origins of museum dioramas

*Wunderkammer* ("wonder rooms" or "cabinets of curiosity"), late Renaissance → a place to show off your unicorn horn, your shrunken head from the Amazon, your really good painting of a hunting dog → Enlightenment: let's figure out where electricity *really* comes from, in case it is not just Devil flames shooting out of a witch's anus → rise of international alliances and colonial conquest → after their years abroad, repatriating ex-pats bring back tiger-skin rugs and boar-tusk bracelets to authenticate (and fetishize) global travel → safaris, porters, gunboat diplomacy and gun-barrel tourism → at the same time, safari taxidermy began to get really good → big cities began to build big, encyclopedic museums (e.g. the Met, in New York, 1870; NHM London's present site, 1880; NHM LA, 1913) → habitat-based concepts of ecological life zones began to take hold in biology departments, so it was not enough to have a stuffed polar bear; one should show in which eco-zones the polar bear best thrives → the Victorians believed that one must educate the masses, and, taking a cue from the stained-glass narrative of Gothic cathedrals, began to see that unnarrated, stand-alone, glow-in-the-dark tableaux could do this (since previously, the richies toured museums with personal guides, pointing and explaining, so no wall labels were needed). So: good stuffed animals + rise in habitat ecology + plus didactic intent = diorama. We had other cultural forces (history-themed cycloramas/panoramas, 1820s–1860s; stereoscope viewers in every parlor, 1860s–1890s; magic lantern slide shows during public lectures; even the drama-filled illustrations of John James Audubon), but the rise of hyperrealistic taxidermy happened to coincide with colonial-era access to exotic game and a general philanthropic ideal to offer up brief pulses of education to the general masses.

### my childhood keeps trying to send me memories

—but they all burn up, coming through the atmosphere. When was the first time I went to the natural history museum, the zoo, the pet store, the La Brea Tar Pits? Can't be sure. I know I was at these places when young, but the memories slide in and out of focus. According to snapshots, I was taken to Watts Towers when I was six months old, then again when I was in sixth grade. It is a complicated thing, returning to sites of personal history as an adult, and going to museums now, I can't be entirely sure I even remember what I think I remember. How to become the person we are intended to become: as a child I went to the zoo; I went to see

*Jungle Book* (the first one, animated); I went to NHM LA where I saw a leopard in a darkened case: a twilight scene, animals in the jungle, and then I dreamed about it that same night. Since then I have been to the jungle many times—dreaming of that childhood leopard before the trips, after them, and probably even during them.

## how come you never talk to me like that

Words culled from articles and books about NHM dioramas: art, beauty, breathtaking, brilliant, Eden, expertise, grand, grandeur, infinite, Louvre, majesty, marvel, masterpiece, Mona Lisa, passion, profound, science, sculptural, Sistine Chapel, spectacular, splendor, startling, theatrical, treasure, unique, valuable, vibrant, Wagnerian, wonder.

## particle physics, continued

For too many years I was a frantic electron orbiting the intense, burning idea of tigers. I went to India to see them, I went to zoos here and abroad, I sought out any second-tier nature center that might have a tatty stuffed one hidden in the gloom of a corner. If there is a tiger book published in the last 150 years, I probably own it. A tiger's skull is dense and broad—firm anchor points for the jaw muscles—and when you lift it out of a museum storage box, you have to hold it with both hands. There is the hole where the spinal cord entered, and on the skull dome sometimes the small, neat, script of its accession number, written in ink. I did indeed feel like I was holding a holy object, albeit a relic with teeth as long as my thumbs. How easily these teeth, these jaws, could clamp down on an ox's neck and crush its windpipe. Even now I am halfway in love with that mouth, can imagine myself dying inside of it. On one museum visit I was allowed to handle a tiger's pelt—what is called in the trade a "study skin"—and the fur was dense, pliable, almost soft. It felt like it would make a high-quality watercolor brush. I was seated with the hide spread out before me on a lab table. Lovely north light coming through cobwebby, third-floor windows. Running the pelt through my hands, I stopped, perplexed. There was—a tear? A defect in the hide? Oh no, had I *broken the tiger??* Not only would they throw me out, they would probably cancel my teacher's discount on my membership. And then as I traced the gap and put a finger through it, it clicked: this was the bullet's entry point. In a diorama mount, the animal's wounds are always filled in or combed over. Even an apprentice taxidermist can make a bullet hole disappear. Not intended for public display, this skin was just as it was when it left the tiger—intact except for the wound in its side, like a murder victim, like a dream, like Christ on the cross, pierced by the Lance of Longinus.

## *my favorite photograph*

When I go to museums, I like to photograph dioramas. Instead of going along with the posed fantasy that these animals really are in nature, I try to include the other visitors or signage or reflections in the glass—something to capture the contradictory feelings that sit in my stomach, or, worse, rise like the slow magma of acid reflux. One of my favorite shots captures an alert group of mule deer. We're at the Grand Canyon, just below the rim; pine trees frame the herd as noble scenery recedes into the purple distance. The central figure, a buck with rippling muscles and a massive rack, has paused to contemplate something located just above our heads. Three lady deer await his instructions stage left; a subordinate male waits stage right, lingering in the wings like the bit player he so clearly is. On the day I got my best photo, California had just ended two weeks of extra-heavy rain. NHM LA dates from 1913, and sometimes the ceiling leaks; if it rains a lot, the ceiling leaks a lot. Trying to air things out, curators had partially raised the glass partition, which lifts like a sash window. The assembled diorama contents included two pine trees, some sagebrush, a few small oaks, three pinyon jays, five mule deer, and one white extension cord snaking into the exhibit from an out-of-exhibit wall outlet, a cord needed to run a small fan inserted into the diorama foreground. It swung slowly right, paused, swung slowly left, paused, then swung back. If you listened, you could hear the whir. The main hero of the scene was no longer the guardian buck; it was the plucky Walmart fan trying its best to dry out the entire Grand Canyon. I vote to leave it there permanently.

### *teddy roosevelt goes to africa*

Creating NHM dioramas was and is an act of intentionality: one needs to go out and get the raw ingredients, then hand it all over to the trompe l'oeil background painters and leaf artisans and hide sewers and antler polishers. Post-presidency, Teddy Roosevelt led a safari to Africa. On behalf of the Smithsonian, the expedition killed ("collected") 5,013 mammals, 4,453 birds, and 2,322 reptiles and amphibians. One would like to think that what was gained (knowledge) was worth the cost (the lives of these organisms). But knowledge is not magically universal: it has to be curated, housed, protected, and that means some groups benefit more than others. The results from this particular trip were indeed data rich, but did the expedition have consent from the indigenous inhabitants to cull such wide swaths of wildlife? Probably not, though the trip would have needed export permits from a district commissioner, so some formalities must have been followed. The basic exchange, though, was one-sided: animals from place x on the globe now are dead at place y. That means that in a larger sense of who takes what from whom, dioramas remind us of previous violations it would be convenient to ignore.

### dioramas as my childhood art practice

As a kid I built model airplanes and Saturn Vs, but my favorite subject was World War II tanks, the Shermans and Tigers and Russian T-34s from the so-called last good war. I liked all sides equally; even now I can tell a German Panzer III from a Mark IV at a glance, though I am embarrassed to admit that out loud. In the conventions of the genre, one worked at 1/35th scale, and the painted, shell-scarred, made-to-look-real models were installed on a landscaped plaque. My intended mise-en-scène might be a farmyard in Italy or the Normandy beachhead, or once, in an experiment that didn't work out, the undersea world of Truk Lagoon. (Allied air raids sank Japanese cargo ships in tropical ports; on those ships were tanks waiting to be deployed; the tanks are there still, under-water, slowly crusting over with coral. *National Geographic* had run an inspiring photospread.) Default shrubbery for other kids was lichen from model railroads. Not me: that looked too fake. I worked hard to construct beeches and oaks and fences and hedgerows that had botanical and historical legitimacy. In the end, I spent more time on the tread marks in the paper-mâché mud than I did on the pleated tracks of the treads themselves. Misplaced emphasis and first taste of how poorly I fit into the world. In the local club's monthly contests, my tanks never won prizes.

## dioramas as art

During my own version of a gentleman's Grand Tour, I have tried to connect most of the NHM dots. That includes the Smithsonian, the Field Museum in Chicago, American NHM in New York, Academy of Sciences in Philadelphia, Iziko in Cape Town, Muséum d'Histoire Naturelle in Paris, NHM London, and NHM LA. If taxi-dermy is art, these are its most vaulted cathedrals. ART: wow, such a big claim for anything, let alone a stuffed hippopotamus standing in plastic mud. Yet these scenes meet most definitions. (1) Display of virtuoso skill/craft. (2) Composition: balance: rule of thirds. (3) Worthy of a repeat visit, prolonged study. (4) Inspires new work and hence helps to extend the cultural conversation. (5) Makes viewers—some of them, some of the time—uncomfortable. Fran-cis Bacon believed that "the job of the artist is always to deepen the mystery." (6) Departures: we can escape the quotidian when we are doing dioramas attentively. Critic Peter Schjeldahl was asked, "What is art for?" He answered, "Vacations from myself." (7) Also: "To delight and instruct," per Horace. (8) If there are small, dull, unambitious diorama scenes, so what. There are loads of utterly mundane, snore-fest landscapes and baskets of Dutch fruit and proforma altarpieces filling the walls in the world's art museums, and that fact does not lessen the power or value of the best art, the real art. (9) Damien Hirst's tiger shark in formaldehyde is a diorama waiting to happen. (10) Just as it is naive to say of a Jackson Pollock abstraction, "My kid could have done that," the NHM diorama itself manipulates perspective in a way no camera lens can achieve. You can buy Nikon's most expensive lens—$16,000 won't even cover the bar tab—and even so, these are still not scenes you will ever photograph on safari in Kenya. In the usual diorama we have a slice of f/22 depth of field in the foreground, with everything in sharp focus for the visual equivalent of the first ten feet or so. But then somehow the middle ground just vanishes—where or how, it's hard to say—and when the background returns, now it is softer, wider, more painterly. You can create that background effect in a panorama camera with the right lens, and if you have good luck with the sunset, but not at the same time as having detail in the initial part of the image, and not without having some distracting middle ground cluttering up the scene. The diorama's lighting too is manipulated and cinematic, even if done with such subtlety viewers rarely notice. True skies under a real sun slosh light around with a sloppy generosity; only inside a portrait studio does the light hit the side of the sitter's face just so. That is to say, a diorama is the 3D version of Velázquez, *Las Meninas*, just with vines and bushes instead of a court dwarf and curtains.

## the hidden longevity of dioramas

When it comes to dioramas themselves, successive museum directors have to leave them alone. Once you have a hall of mammals installed, that's all she wrote. You can hold banquets in the space or swap out one animal for another, but in general, it is there for the duration. In a regular art museum, works get loaned out, works get stolen, works get sent away for cleaning or they get deaccessioned or that era falls out of vogue and new trends line the walls. If an artwork achieves too much prominence it has to go behind a cordon and a pane of bulletproof glass. The art that everyone knows and loves is safe from removal, but in the rest of the museum, most art is unreliable; fall in love with a painting and sooner or later it will break your heart. Not true for a stuffed giraffe, legs splayed, neck down, drinking. Once you have discovered the natural history museum's African waterhole, go ahead and settle down to enjoy it all you want, because it can't ever be put in storage.

## i almost got my hopes up there for a moment

A few years ago the Field Museum crowdfunded a diorama for hyenas in Somalia, based on specimens collected in 1896. (They installed the diorama in the hall for Mammals of Asia, some geographical funny business, but at least it's better than the hyenas' prior location in the Hall of Reptiles.) The appeal worked; 1,500 donors helped fund the creation of the new diorama. Sadly, I misread the press release, and thought the diorama was going to show the real Somalia, the *current* Somalia. I wanted accurate natural history but also accurate political history, so I pictured a scene with stony ground, acacia scrub, endemic birds like a Somali lark or lesser hoopoe-lark, the hyenas of course, maybe a bit of rubbish and barbed wire, and, instead of boulders or a waterhole for the main structure, a burned-out hull of a white UN armored car. I wanted my Panzer days to make friends with my NHM days. Not ever going to happen—dream on, poet boy, dream on.

### meet me behind the animal hall in ten minutes

People who work in museums hook up, same as at any workplace. Not supposed to, but it happens. And meanwhile, some dioramas have access panels from the service corridor. So which NHM has a hollow space inside a cliff, a space not much bigger than a phone booth, where staff can go for a quick rendezvous? All of them, I hope.

### we are all victorians at heart

One problem with NHM dioramas—and to reiterate again, I love them dearly, and they remain my favorite part of the museum—is the limited range of possibilities the convention allows. One artist did a landfill diorama with trash and gulls, but it never got past the art gallery. No museum would consider it. In NHM LA there's a very risky exhibit, newish, that shows a coyote with a dead cat in its mouth. A feral parrot looks on. The point is to show what I call blended nature, the intersection of native species (coyotes) and human-supplied ones (cats, parrots). The parrot is fine, but a dead cat? How did that make it past approval committees? This is an exception to the general rules of diorama making. We don't see coyotes scent marking, lions humping, gay penguins sharing pebbles in a colony, or even the simple reality of a skinning table in a field camp, as ornithology grad students prepare just-shot specimens to ship back home. Poachers do not set snares in the rain forests that populate NHMs, and plastic Coke bottles don't float downstream. We follow our elders in this; the most popular Victorian art told clear moral lessons while excluding unseemly details.

## so which is it, particle or wave?

At my home museum, NHM LA, the one I grew up in and am a member of now, the African waterhole scene is mesmerizing—it even has elephant dung and birds and convincing yellow grass crackling in the imagined heat. There is a railing but no glass, and the scene must be thirty feet wide. Giraffes browse and elephants wander, and the view immerses you in habitat and verisimilitude. The cape buffalo even peer around fluted woodwork of the frame, breaking the fourth wall by looking out at the visitors in the hall, calmly chewing cud, bemused by the sight of us. But that seemingly "true" scene describes an Africa that does not exist, and in fact is a scene that never existed, or if it existed, existed in ways I don't want anything to do with. Anytime on a safari, even a scientific safari, when the servants have no choice but to say, "Yes, Bwana," and fetch you another gin and tonic, then the c-word, colonialism, hovers over the encounter like a lingering cloud of poison gas. A statue looted from a tomb or a painting stolen from a Jewish dealer in Paris in 1944 or an Aztec codex painted under duress to please an occupying army, those objects can never be divorced from their points of origin nor scrubbed clean of their illicit transfers. Context matters, history matters, the way in which science happens and is transmitted matters. True art can withstand intense scrutiny, and if Lynyrd Skynyrd or Stevie Nicks can handle the honesty and muckraking of VH1's *Behind the Music*, NHMs (and their visitors and curators and trustees and guidebook authors) can afford to take an equally honest look at past conventions and current practices. Perhaps we just need to be as noble and stoic as the displays themselves. After all, they are doing the best they can, these poor stuffed animals. They look out at us from the well-lit glass, as if to say, "We know where *we* belong. We know our home range and native habitat. It is all around us every day, frozen in time, and it will not change. What about you, dear viewer? Do you know where *you* belong?"

# Cochineal and the Color Red

I have always been fond of cactus. At first I was attracted to its proudly contrarian nature—ugly shape, nasty spines, and if you don't like it, fine then, go hike someplace else—but I loved it even more once I learned that cactus has had more impact on European and American culture than any other New World plant—more than the avocado, the banana, the maize ear, and the chili pepper.

The particular cactus under review is the prickly pear, genus Opuntia. Rounding up, we might guestimate the total species list at one hundred, all native only to North and South America. There are hybrids and blends and one-offs as well, which means that in California, prickly pear is both a native plant and an introduced plant, and, as a cultivar, both a food crop and a garden ornamental.

Most species of Opuntia can host the cochineal, a parasite

whose infestations make the cactus pads look like they have been spackled with crusty toothpaste. When scraped off the cactus pad, dried, and pressed into cakes, cochineal creates a carmine dye that was Spain's most lucrative export from the Americas, second only to silver and far ahead of sugar, vanilla, cotton, tobacco, gold, and sisal. Starting in the 1520s, cochineal dye was traded globally, and after the Spanish empire collapsed, it made native growers in Oaxaca rich, and their clients, the Dutch and Venetian dye masters, richer still.

The story starts with Cortés. It is easy to call the conquistadores ruthless, bloodthirsty colonizers (because that's exactly what they were), but contra Neil Young's song "Cortez the Killer," they had not waltzed into a cheery, blissful Eden. Can you love a song but mock its lyrics? According to Mr. Young, in the world of Montezuma, "Hate was just a legend / And war was never known / The people worked together / And they lifted many stones." Nice scene, but utter balderdash. Better to go with A. A. Gill: "It's a great historical joke that when the Spanish met the Aztecs, it was a blind date made in serve-you-right heaven. At the time, they were the two most unpleasant cultures in the entire world, and richly deserved each other. Still, the story of how stout Cortés blustered, bullied, and bludgeoned his way to collapsing an entire empire with a handful of contagious hoodlums is astonishing."

The Spanish didn't invent cochineal harvesting, but they

did commandeer the recipe—and take over acres and acres of cultivated prickly pear. Preconquest, cochineal had been used in South America for royal capes and in Mesoamerica as a paint for codices. As soon as it arrived in Europe, dyers began to experiment wildly. Mix it with arsenic? That produces a rich cinnamon. Urine salts? Nope, they dinge it down to weak gray, and everybody had plenty of that. Tin makes it brightest yet. As formulas developed, it turned out that cochineal could bind equally well to wool, silk, or linen, and, with the right mordants, it became brighter and more insanely red. It was also used for cosmetics (lipstick, cheek rouge) and, occasionally, as medicine—can cochineal cure whooping cough? Some treatises thought so.

Welcome to the era of cochineal, the red that out-reds everything else, the red that starts as insects on cactus. The red that when dried and cooked and mixed with this and that lit up the sixteenth and seventeenth centuries like sunlight after a dreary winter. According to one account, British women even outlined their nipples in red; a different source insists it was not British women, but French.

To meet demand, Spain oversaw cochineal farms stretching from Txlaxcala to Chile. By the end of the sixteenth century, cochineal was being used in Japan and China. Emily Dickinson wrote about it and Byron did too, and El Greco, Zurbarán, Van Dyck, and Van Gogh all painted with it. When Diego Velázquez finished *Las Meninas* in 1656, dim in the gloom are floor-to-ceiling red drapes, since Philip IV's status and cochineal-derived wealth allowed him the luxury of cochineal-dyed fabric on an immense scale. You could buy a Lamborghini for what one of those drapes cost. Vatican cardinals buttoned on cochineal when electing a new pope. British redcoats marched cochineal-dyed wool uniforms across the village greens of Lexington and Concord, Boston and Albany, Yorktown and Saratoga. One of cochineal's virtues as a dye, besides being vivid and indelible, is that it is consistent. If you want to batch-dye large quantities of fabric and create uniform uniforms, this is the stuff for you.

You can try it out for yourself. Just find a stand of cactus and then look for the fuzzy white stuff that splotches the skin of the cactus paddles. (It can also cover the *tuna*, or red cactus fruit.) Once you have found the white crust, take a Swiss Army Knife and smoosh a small patch with the broad side of the blade. The result is a small puddle of intense carmine. Just be sure to clean the blade off with a leaf or piece of tissue—if you wipe it on your jeans, you'll be left with a stain that commemorates the experiment forever.

All of this high-voltage color starts with an insect smaller than a grain of rice. It lives in parasitic colonies on the skin of a cactus, taking a tithe of water and nutrients but usually not causing lethal harm. Three species live in California, including the kind that was harvested for dye in Mexico, *Dactylopius coccus.* As a substance, it puzzled early naturalists. Was it a worm? A kind of grain? What part of the cactus did it grow on? Not until microscopes became a thing in the late seventeenth century did the insect's body and lifestyle get a preliminary review. Quick version is that the lady cochineal lives her life in one place and has lots of eggs; the young ones move around for a few weeks then finally settle down. At that point, they do what mama does: create a white, waxy coating; develop a red acid that's toxic to most things that want to eat them; drill down with a needle mouth, and parasitize the cactus for the rest of their sessile lives. (There is a male insect, but it has no red.) All goes on in harmony for one year or a hundred years until too many cochineal colonies taking too much cactus sap kills the host plant, or until a gentle swish of a whisk broom harvests the cochineal into a jar to be dried in the sun, mixed with clay, pressed into cakes, and shipped around the world to later be reconstituted into premium-grade, ultrared dye.

"There is red, and then there is *red*, the color of vixen lips and midlife crisis." So explains historian of color Carolyn Purnell. Want to announce the end of the drab, worn-out Middle Ages and drumroll in the new kid on the block, the Renaissance? Cochineal will do it. As Purnell says, red is "the color that Louis XIV wore on his heels to prove that he could crush his enemies easily. It's the color that Christian Louboutin puts on the soles of his signature stilettos, so women can announce, in a flash, their luxury and style. It's the color that often shows up on va-va-voom dresses and that gives its name to those districts where illicit pleasures find expression." She goes on to note that while it is true that "red does sometimes invite us closer," more often, "it stops us in our tracks. Stop signs were originally yellow, but American standardizers realized that the color wasn't immediate enough. Red is urgent. It's the color of focus. It's an insistent *now now now*."

Pre-cochineal, some red came from cinnabar, aka mercury sulfide, and some came from madder, a type of root plant, but Europe generally rendered red from the lac insect, *Kerria lacca*. It was red, but not *that* red. When something else came along, everybody was glad to change teams. The process even touched literature. A visionary poet, Christopher Smart, included the scale insect in his multipage celebration of God:

Let Ramah rejoice with Cochineal.
*For H is a spirit and therefore he is God.*

Let Gaba rejoice with the Prickly Pear, which the
Cochineal feeds on.
*For I is a person and therefore he is God.*

The garrison flag flying over Fort McHenry in "The Star-Spangled Banner" had its semiotic, lasting-through-the-night stripes thanks to the alchemy of Mexican insects. In the Southwest, nineteenth-century Navajo textile artists unraveled trade cloth to reuse the red-dyed wool, reweaving the color into their own stories and symbols.

Commodities rise and fall, and after the arrival of artificial dyes and a glut due to pirate cochineal from the Canary Islands and elsewhere, Mexico's Opuntia fields went fallow. Yet all that was old will be new again someday, and cochineal is back, as an organic and artisanal product (and as the name of a trendy restaurant in Marfa, Texas). Designers are using cochineal for modern ball gowns, and once more, weavers and dyers are turning to it for colors and shades no synthetics can match. Its appeal shines as brightly today as it did when the first Europeans sailed their barnacle-encrusted, bilge-leaking, deeply unquarantined ships into the pristine bays and lagoons of the New World.

That is why I recommend that cochineal red should be California's official state color. And I nominate Opuntia too—cactus and cactus worm together, for endurance, for humility, for the contrast of what is hidden versus what is revealed, for the pleasure of grilled *nopales* with Corona and lime, for the *tuna* fruit that makes such fine jelly on bagels. What a tough-ass plant the cactus is, and how strange and marvelous are the cochineal scales. Together, they are a cage for sunrise. Together, *Who needs rain?* Together, like us, they are a dance older than history.

*Booby Gannet*
SULA FUSCA.

Drawn from Nature by J. J. Audubon, F.R.S. F.L.S.

Engraved, Printed, & Coloured, by R. Havell, 1834.

# Audubon's Tiny Houses

He could dance, sing, draw, shoot, ride, sew, fence, and play the flute. In London he wore buckskins; on the frontier, white linen. John Keats called him a fool. Harry Truman collected his art, as did Queen Victoria, Roger Tory Peterson, Mark Twain, and Charles Darwin's extended family. He admired Indians but owned nine enslaved people. He went bankrupt often. In 2010 a copy of his book sold at Sotheby's for $11.5 million. Despite factual reality—that he was born in Haiti, the illegitimate son of a slave-owning pirate and a chambermaid who maybe was white, maybe mixed-race—at times he claimed he was the son of a hero from the American Revolution. After kissing the Blarney Stone especially hard, he claimed he was none other than the lost Dauphin, heir to the throne of France. He also claimed to have been taught art by the Neoclassical master Jacques-Louis David.

Nice try, Mr. Audubon, but all three stories are as false as George Washington's front teeth.

Art history does not waste much time on John James Audubon (1785–1851), though the critic Robert Hughes aligns him with Gilbert Stuart, Grant Wood, Mark Rothko, and Andy Warhol. Hughes is the exception; in the 1,100 pages of Gardner's *Art through the Ages,* Monsieur Audubon is mentioned a grand total of zero times. Yet a dozen towns are named after him, several historical parks, some bridges, a major nature society, one shearwater, a small rabbit, an extinct ram, a warbler, and an oriole. Audubon did not found the Audubon Society (named *for* him, not *by* him); what he did do, though, is create *Birds of America,* and *Birds of America* is, let it be clear, just about the greatest nature book ever made.

Audubon was never not working, and even though he wrote ornithology handbooks and painted mammals and discovered new species like the Bell's vireo and the black-footed ferret, none of that matters, those things are twigs and pebbles compared to his stupendous idea, his stupendous folly, *Birds of America.* This book—more a serial edition of prints, really—weighs sixty pounds when all the elements are stacked together in one pile. Inside it you can find every species of bird in the then-United States and territories, plus a few that he got wrong—so, *more* than every species. Six of them are now extinct, gone forever except for his plates and tattered specimens. Each bird has been drawn lovingly, precisely, and implausibly at true-to-life-size scale. To achieve this goal he had to use paper whose trim size, 39.5 x 28.5 inches, is usually called "double elephant."

Nobody had seen a nature book like this before. *Life-size*— how utterly bonkers. Just to make it even more challenging, he often included representative plants, or in the case of owls and raptors, samples of typical prey. From hummingbirds to the full-pouched white pelican, the ratio stayed the same, even if that meant embedding sparrows in a tangle of botany surrounded by a sea of negative space. At the other end of the scale, Audubon had to fold the tallest things in half to get them to fit. If you don't know his plan, his flamingo might look like a zoo escapee who got splinched trying to fax itself to freedom.

Over the course of twenty years, Audubon crafted 435 finished plates. He was motivated by the same thing that drove Shakespeare and Courbet and Thomas Edison: he did it because he had to. It burned in him to do it, but he also did it to make a living. The book was a commercial enterprise; Audubon made art not for art's sake, but for it-puts-food-on-the-table sake. Yet as a project, not a single day was easy. To get his editions engraved, printed, colored, and distributed, he had to leave America and go to England, and even there it took several tries to find the right collaborators. The Havells, *père et fils,* ended up needing fifty assistants to help color all the finished plates. By the time the second edition was ready—smaller size, cheaper price—the plate count had grown to five hundred. Audubon also wrote a five-volume companion text, *Ornithological Biographies*, and near the end of his life he started a series on mammals. He died before it was finished; his sons and a friend named Bachman finished it for him.

Manufacture of the giant bird book was a multistep process. First he had to locate, identify, acquire, and compose the species in question. One art historian, rather than using the expression "life-size" (given that the birds were, at time of being drawn and painted, already dead), prefers to call Audubon's practice "actual-size drawing." Once a painting was ready, it was copied as a reversed image onto a copper plate. The plate was dipped in acid, rinsed, inked, and turn-screwed to very big paper. Then that paper, once printed, was hand colored. Finished pages were issued in sets and sold by subscription to people with good taste, large houses, and wheelbarrows of disposable income. Reviewing a modern edition, Alexander Nazaryan asks, "Is it the most beautiful book ever produced? I don't know: Was Helen the most beautiful woman in ancient Greece? The Gutenberg Bible probably played a bigger role in the history of Western civilization, but Audubon's work feels more alive."

When Audubon began *Birds of America*, nobody knew all the

birds yet, not even his late rival, Alexander Wilson. As a space, "America" was so new the paint was still wet—that is, white America, gringo America, was new; Audubon lived through (but did not comment on) the Trail of Tears. When he started, the precise borders of the Louisiana Purchase still had not been negotiated. People hunted with old-style flintlock muskets— one reason bison and passenger pigeons lasted as long as they did. Signers of the Declaration of Independence were still alive; Daniel Boone and Davy Crockett were Audubon's contemporaries.

Eighteen-year-old Audubon had come to America not to paint but to dodge the draft. Though he had been born in the Caribbean, he was raised in France. With Napoleon needing every young man to do his duty and die for his country, conscription looked inevitable. In 1803 Audubon found himself on a ship for New York, traveling with a forged passport. (Thanks, Papa.) Somewhere in that transformation he learned a Quaker-influenced English and his name changed from Jean-Jacques Fougère to simple and direct John James. A long middle period arises in which he gets married, launches and fails at various businesses, has children, some of whom die, and finally ends up starting *Birds of America*. Who gave him permission even to try? Perhaps William Blake came to him in a vision. The great influx of Japanese woodblock prints into Western art world hadn't yet happened, and so without direct models, Audubon had to invent

*Chinoiserie* and *Japonisme* (and late Matisse and the graphic clarity of *Saturday Evening Post*) all on his mad own. Yet just about every page of *Birds of America* works, and when it doesn't—we'll get to his hunchbacked, dolorous, infinitely black California condor in a moment—it often fails in interesting ways.

Did I mention he could dance? What a catch he was, so long as you don't mind dating men who get up at 3:00 a.m. and come home wearing coats smeared with cornmeal and blood. In the late portraits he looks aquiline and regal, with such gorgeous hair he could have starred in ads for shampoo. He was tall for the time, trim, somebody who had kept his good looks and knew it. He must have missed speaking French, and we know he treasured the Cajun names for birds. Thanks to him we remember that the snipe was called a *cache-cache*, while the indigo bunting was *petit papebleu*. What Audubon called the tell-tale godwit and sometimes yellowshanks (what we know now as the greater yellowlegs) was a *clou-clou* in Cajun, based on an onomatopoeic transcription of the alarm call. Nothing went to waste in early America, and if you shot birds to draw them, you ate them afterwards, or at least tried to. While young *clou-clou* can be tasty, he reported, "in general, these birds are thin and have a fishy taste."

Audubon practiced lifelong sobriety, a virtuous path that made no difference because the arsenic he used for preserving bird skins was killing him daily, hourly. Everybody used it, is the thing; his name is one of many on a list of people who risked poison in the pursuit of science. One nineteenth-century manual of ornithology cheerfully explains that "arsenic is a good friend of ours; besides preserving birds, it keeps busybodies and meddlesome folks away from the scene of operations." How should it be stored? "It may be kept in the tin pots in which it is usually sold; but a shallower, broader receptacle is more convenient." The directions for how to build a drawer into one's worktable are given next, so you can have your arsenic immediately at hand. You also will need a salt spoon borrowed from the kitchen ("or a little wooden shovel whittled like one") and of course a selection of scalpels.

All of Audubon's birds inhabit spatial ambivalence, since they are expected to be accurate demonstrations of literal species—DNA and syrinx, rectrix and appetite—and yet also graphic designs filling the page. The two tasks should repel each other like same-pole magnets. Somehow they don't, and often one is treated to an intense vitality: an Audubon tern in flight looks so taut it could be an archer's loaded bow. When the release snaps, the bird won't merely zoom off the page, it will end up in the next county. The variety of pose and variety of color and style mean that finding a favorite plate is not hard. Most top-ten lists will include one of the egrets or herons, one of the moments of tender domesticity (doves are always popular), and one of the scenes of high drama—maybe rattlesnake versus mockingbird, maybe the moths against the whippoorwills, or maybe Plate CCXLI, the black-backed gull, who, wing up, dying, manages to embody all the pathos of a first-rate *Pietà*. One art critic sees that plate as being echoed, slash for slash, by a particularly intense Franz Kline abstract.

Fine as these examples are, I prefer the queer, unsuccessful plates, especially CCCCXVI, the one showing a bird Audubon called the "California vulture"—accurate enough name, though today we call it the California condor. (The word *condor* came into English in Shakespeare's time, transferred via Spanish, which had borrowed it from Quechua.) Lewis and Clark knew condors and John Muir saw them over Pasadena, but as the twentieth century rolled on, they ate lead shot and flew into electrical wires and drank radiator fluid and queued up for the greased slide to extinction. In a Hail Mary pass, in 1987 the last twenty-two free-flying California condors were captured, put in pens, shown some vulturine porn, and encouraged to multiply like fruit flies. A bit to everybody's surprise, they did just that, and reintroduced condors are now back in the sky in California, Utah, Arizona, and Baja. They show up near Gorman sometimes, and by the east side of Pinnacles National Park. You can see them in Big Sur and Zion and Sequoia and the Grand Canyon. Good job, team. By the time this goes to press, the wild population will have passed five hundred.

To make his sketches, Audubon didn't use a camera—nobody did, they were just being invented—and so to draw a bird he had to hold a bird, or at least have it hanging from wires in front of him. For this condor plate, Audubon's specimen came from a man named Townsend, for whom a warbler and a solitaire are named. (Townsend died at forty-one of arsenic poisoning.) Audubon had not seen the condor alive, despite the folio's caption "drawn from life," and that may explain why he struggled to give it a defined posture. Looking at it now, it is hard to tell if it is sad or just has a stiff neck. The white wing flash is painted in with great precision, but makes the middle of the wing look like a sideways piano. If you were painting condors today, you would probably include their plastic wing tags, since most condors wear color-coded badges to help researchers track them in flight. If you spot a wild condor, grab a picture, and you can look up who it is. Red 67, for example, identifies Kingpin, born in 1997 and the boss of the Big Sur condor flock. At a kill, he claims first dibs. According to his bio on the web, "Kingpin paired with condor #190 in 2006 and they established a breeding territory that spring. In 2007, the pair started nesting in the cavity of a coast redwood tree." Condors in a redwood: two Pleistocene survivors in one view.

Wing disks remind us that even the Sublime has to

accommodate the semiotics of allegiance and order. At the track, a jockey's silks are keyed to his sponsor's stable; during a marathon, runners' bibs confer identity. Some people don't like to see nature overwritten by the reality of human intervention, but from radio collars on pumas to a highway sign warning to watch out for desert tortoises, what we value most outdoors often first had to be studied or managed before it was recognized as worthy of preservation. In doing their jobs, sometimes the puppeteers can't completely hide the strings.

Audubon did not have to deal with plastic number tags or aluminum leg bands, but he did have trouble with the condor's neck ruff, which looks bedraggled and askew—Phyllis Diller has a costume bathrobe with a boa like that. He did a better job with the head, which on a condor is bare (as it is on most vultures), since they have to stick their heads deep into putrid carcasses, and matted feathers would attract lice. Mostly, though, this is a study of black on black; not only is the immense slab of the bird entirely dark, but so is the cross-branch it perches on.

With this plate, size matters. Almost all good art looks more interesting in person. If you look up the condor plate on a phone or tablet it won't seem like much, but at the Huntington Library in San Marino or the University of Pittsburgh or the Beinecke Library at Yale—places where you can linger over original editions—once you experience the condor plate at full folio size, hang on to the railing, because it sucks the air out of you all the way down to your ankles. Black bird, black branch, huge page, clean white background: I will see your Franz Kline and raise you two Rothko Chapels and a Black Flag poster. At home, leafing through my much-smaller trade edition, pages like the condor's provide necessary pause after a swirl of overamped parakeets or the maudlin drama of an eagle capping a hare.

Some people think the condor looks glum, even menacing. It's all the black, I suppose. If this were a three-foot-tall blue jay, nobody would mind. Kassia St. Clair, in her book *The Secret Lives of Color*, says that "a whiff of death has clung to black as far back as records reach, and humans are fascinated and repelled by it. Most of the gods associated with death and the underworld are depicted with truly black skin, and the color has long been associated with both mourning and witchcraft." She could have also mentioned the Puritans, who were nobody's idea of cheerful.

Values evolve, and during Audubon's lifetime, black became more fashionable. Cultural historian Michel Pastoureau talks about changes in theatrical performances and costuming that started in the 1820s. "Hamlet, especially, became a Romantic hero, and his famous black costume, a veritable uniform, was more in keeping with the sensibility and style of the era than [Goethe's] Werther's sensible blue suit, henceforth totally obsolete." Black soon spread to the sartorial expectations of the average man. "The phenomenon began in the last years of the eighteenth century, grew during the French Revolution—an honest citizen had to wear a black suit—triumphed in the Romantic period, lasted throughout the nineteenth century, and only exhausted itself in the 1920s." For women, black may have been given a fashion boost by Queen Victoria, who wore black for forty years of widowhood.

In some grids, black is not even a real color (since it is all the colors). Novice painters learn that the least convincing way to paint something black is to use black paint right out of the tube—better to mix blue into orange, try that way. At the end of his life, Francisco Goya made his Black Paintings, fourteen bleak visions muraled directly onto the walls of a house. Audubon and Goya were contemporaries separated by an ocean of circumstance. The atrocities and crimes of the Napoleonic Wars had worn Goya out, and these are dark works—dark in hue, dark in theme. The grim *Saturn Devouring His Son* would have been painted in blood, except blood isn't black enough.

Audubon has his own sharp edges. Why do his quadrupeds look so mean—even his beavers snarl like rabid wolves—and in plate after plate, why are there so many life-and-death struggles? His art reflected the times but also his own hopes, dreams, traumas, and inspirations. Audubon was born on a sugar plantation in the Caribbean. His father was a privateer turned slave dealer and plantation owner. After Audubon's mother died, his next mother was another of his father's mixed-race mistresses. His father then left Haiti and went back to France, where he reconciled with his back-at-the-farm original wife. On the eve of the Haitian Slave Revolt, he brought Audubon and a half-sister to live with him in France. During these dislocations and relocations, Audubon lived through successive layers of loss and doubt. He may have been too young to hear much about the uprising in Haiti, but he would have seen firsthand the horror show of the French Revolution. His father took the legal steps to legitimize him, and then sent him to join the dreamers in America. Audubon never saw his French family again.

In America, was Audubon a person of color passing as white in a slave-owning country? His racial status seems relevant, even urgent, but we cannot be certain. Some scholars think they have traced his biological mother back to a white woman born in France, but on the other hand, when he was born, twenty thousand enslaved people a year were being imported to Haiti, some of them by his own father. It seems unlikely that a white French woman would have been needed as a servant on an island with such a casual abundance of mistreated Afro-Carib humanity, but she may have followed a man (or woman) there out of love, or became indentured through no fault of her own, or maybe she just wanted to see what waited past the edge of the known world.

Hold a mirror up to the nineteenth century, and you can see reflected back any reading that you hope to find. Hyphenate as needed: Audubon was a Haitian-American artist, or no, he was more of a French-American, or he was a Failed-at-Business American, or he was a vain, handsome man trying to P. T. Barnum his way into the salons of royalty. We do know he was a naturalist who had not gone to a university and who was not part of the landed gentry. His first mother died of infection and his next mother got left behind on Haiti, perhaps resold, perhaps set free, perhaps left to die in the uprising. All of this had to have touched him; experience leaves its dirty fingerprints on our collars no matter how successful our lives may seem from a distance. Artists make art for many reasons: to document the world and to repudiate the world, to praise color and to violate color, to heal wounds and to inflict them. Audubon the person—not Audubon the coffee mug, Audubon the postage stamp—was a blend of many parts of the palette, not all of them complementary.

Further complicating things, we have the stark reality that each and every page required a small act of deletion from the tree of life. It would be accurate (but unfair) to create a headstone that reads, "John James Audubon—he sure shot a lot of birds." First, everybody did; second, he put them to such good use, he has a free pass, even for the passenger pigeons. Part of Audubon's genius was how unrestrainedly he worked, freestyling each picture with whatever he had on hand. Audubon wanted his birds to look like birds and did whatever it took to get there, moving back and forth between watercolor, gouache, graphite, pastel, chalk, ink, oil paint, overglazing, metal leaf, and collage. He should have been making illustrations, and instead, by luck or quirk or because he didn't know he wasn't supposed to, he made art.

He also invented a miniature world uncomplicated by race or dead mothers or the sound of the mob shouting the tumbrel up the hill. In and around the birds, behind them and under them and despite them, Audubon's plates reveal hidden farms, distant steeples, raging oceans, vertical cliffs. On one page he might linger to create a detailed study of a gull's foot, a small visual detour floating free of the narrative frame; another scene will lavish adoring attention on weeds and thistles, more so than botanical necessity requires. Not all of this started with his own pencil; over the years he worked with four assistants (one of them a woman who later became his best friend's wife) to complete the backgrounds. Collectively, Team Audubon concocted a magical and separate reality. I especially love Plate 207, "Booby Gannet," since it is a strong vertical composition—the tall, brown bird with a blazing white belly balances on a brown snag, the arch of its neck and beak matched by the outward swoop of the stiff tail.

Yet beneath the solid presence of the dark bird on the dark

stick, pushed down into the bottom 10 percent of the frame, is a calm strip of coastal Florida, where a dozen white houses and outbuildings doze next to a slim pier and scattering of ships at anchor, all beneath pastel bands of summer clouds. The bird's webbed feet end in exquisite toenails (no detail is too small to notice), and then all of the foreground image drops away, revealing an alternate universe in the distant background. Who lives in the nice, large house? Who first planted the sabal palm barely visible between the farthest buildings on the left? Is it somebody's birthday today? The shed on the dock must be full of crab pots and coiled sisal line. The background details become a world within a world. Look closer, pilgrim, and closer still. In the final print, the village palmetto is so small you need a jeweler's loupe to find it.

Audubon's tiny worlds—partly real, partly idealized bucolia that existed only in his own mind—are all the more convincing because he didn't even know he was making them. He would probably be surprised to learn they have received notice at all, and he almost certainly would not be able to explain why he made them or where they came from, emotionally. Plate 347 shows a pair of black-and-white sea ducks from Europe. It is a moody, arctic scene, one with foreground and background, no middle ground. (This is true for most Audubon tableaux.) The caption lets us know these are "Smews or White Nuns." The main duck diagonals top right to bottom left, streaking towards the bottom in Stuka glory. We see him from above, eyes gleaming, black-and-white wings arched into a tight W. A black blaze between his shoulder blades looks like a jetpack or an emergency scuba tank. Already landed, his sorrel-headed mate bobs in a boreal lagoon below, unifying the composition with horizontal body and a head turning to look up and left.

The surface action is nominally required—this is a bird book, after all—but slowly the scene behind the ducks emerges like a harbor coalescing out of the fog. We are in Labrador or New-foundland or a small bay on the coast of Pluto, and the water, the sky, and the gelid coast are equal layers of translucent gray, as if the sea cliffs happen to be pieces of vertical water that got up and went for a walk. It doesn't look fake; instead, it looks so real that one suddenly realizes how much translucence the reg-ular geology books leave out. I have a copy of this plate on my computer, and for fun I tried inverting it. It works even better upside-down. Now the female is on top, clinging to the bottom of the crenulated sky like a bat, while the male sculls through an ocean of silt-gray silk to join her.

In drawing after strange drawing, it was as if Audubon had never seen a book before, or that what he most wanted to be was the first postmodernist at the party, knocking on the host's door 150 years too early. In Plate 171 we learn that barn owls keep dead squirrels as pets and that on evenings with a good moon, they are lit from within, like the windows of all-night diners. Plate 125, brown-headed nuthatch, pretends it is an illustration of two passerines foraging on a branch, but really it wants to be about the bold, vertical Y that dominates the page; the birds are minor afterthoughts, attractive but inconsequential. The true subject is the weathered wood and the way it extends out past the top and bottom of the frame, taking us to a lost world of peeling bark and eternal lichen. The branch owns the page utterly, and the page exists only to present the branch to us, like a velvet pillow indenting to accept the imperial gravitas of the queen's scepter.

Once all the sets had been printed, the copper plates from *Birds of America* were crated up and shipped back to Audubon in America. Before they could be unloaded, the ship sank in New York Harbor. The plates sat in seawater for many months before being salvaged. Once on shore, the warehouse they were being stored in burned down. After Audubon's death in 1851, his widow, burdened by debt, sold what remained for the value of their weight in copper. Somehow—the hand of fate works in strange ways—a few plates survived the scrapper's furnace and are still extant. Audubon State Park in Kentucky owns one: Plate 308, the tell-tale godwits (the ones that don't taste so great).

In 2002 Friends of Audubon, hoping to raise money for conservation, issued what is a called a restrike. Using archival paper, they reinked Plate 308, and for the first time since 1836, new prints were pulled. Fifty were done with black ink and fifty with sepia, and the intent was not to color them, but to let them be clean, stark, and modern (modern except for the faux antiquity of the sepia ink, that is.)

It did not work out. Due to the corruption of the plate, the prints developed an eerie blur, the way one might expect to see the face of a ghost looking back at you from a clouded mirror. To protect the plate, no more restrikes will be issued.

I wish they had tried a bit harder, dared to do just a few more pulls, and then I wish the plate had cracked in two, exploded, detonated, become consumed by fire as thunder crashed out of the clouds and darkness fell upon the hills and fields of Kentucky. Some things should be left alone. Let there be no sequels to *The Great Gatsby* or *Beloved,* no remakes of *Casablanca* or *The Godfather,* no embellishments to Mahler's Ninth, no new characters added to *Hamlet* or *Death of a Salesman.*

We can print anything we want now, at any size and in any color, and yet like the Pleiades rising blue and bright above the horizon, Audubon's *Birds of America* remains a constellation whose exact origins we cannot explain—not merely a nature book but a star cluster whose light, after all these years, is still trying to reach us.

# Landscape with Unicorns and Barnacles

Everybody loves whales. Honey badgers had their meme moment, but there are whale license plates, orca key fobs, tours to San Ignacio Lagoon to go pet the whales. Whales are it.

Initially what we most loved about whales was killing them, and in North America we practiced that love starting in the 1530s, when Basque fishermen first discovered the whale feeding grounds off of Newfoundland. Boat followed boat, harpoon followed harpoon, and in time, the Atlantic populations of gray whale were hunted to extinction. After that there were other choices, including right whales (the "right" whale to hunt), bowhead whales with baleen plates taller than a man, and best of the best, the cachalot or sperm whale, a floating island of money whose boxcar head holds five hundred gallons of creamy wax worth more than frankincense and myrrh. Profits were split by lays or shares: land a few bull sperm whales on a half-year voyage and everybody will get rich, even the cabin boy.

In the typical model, the ship, usually Yankee in origin, goes to the whale, but it can also work the other way around: wait patiently and let the whales swim past. This explains the shore-based whaling stations once found along the California coast, active from the 1850s until the 1880s, with a few crews still going out in 1920. You could find whale operations in Bolinas, at Pigeon Point (later home to the tallest lighthouse on the West Coast), in Monterey and Santa Cruz, in Goleta just north of Santa Barbara, in LA's San Pedro (two bases, including one on what was then called Dead Man's Island), and in San Diego (two bases). There was plenty of beach to go around; if you had the desire and saw an opportunity, nature was there for the taking.

Hard work to kill a whale, so whaling happened for commerce, not malice. Oil for lamps, for lubrication, for the insatiable needs of the Industrial Revolution—at first oil came not from the ground but from chunks of boiled whale. Butchering is the same no matter where the location or what the style of hunting. Spot a whale, chase it in rowed longboats, then harpoon it. The harpoon or "iron" is a toggle-headed spear with a five- or six-foot shaft. A ring on the back end is where you tie a rope that is carefully coiled in a basket. Harpoons don't kill whales; harpoons use the boat as a kind of drogue parachute to wear the whale out. The wounded animal dives (and the rope smokes from heat, flying out of the basket and around a capstan) but eventually it comes up for air, dragging the boat behind it. In time, the crew works close enough to lance the whale in the heart or lungs. Animal dives, surfaces, is lanced; dives, surfaces, is lanced—for as many hours as it takes until it breaks free or dies. If it dies, then tie ropes around the tail and tow. Bring the body alongside a ship or close enough to winch it onto the shore.

Next comes flensing (to cut flesh off in strips) and trying out (to cook the meat and fat in giant caldrons). A sperm whale's head (or "case") holds a special grade of ultrapremium product. If one piece of the ocean is hunted out, go to the next one. American ships sailed to all the corners of the map. If the map didn't exist, they went anyway—Yankee captains were nothing if not persistent—and if the whales dove, they waited an hour and killed them when they came back up, and if they tried to hide in Greenland or Antarctica, we went there too. Let Russia corner the market in sea otter pelts, let Britain chase the international flow of wool, wheat, sugar, butter, silk, rum, tea, and flax, let Spain grow pale and thin eking out the final trickles from its exhausted silver mines, because in the United States in the nineteenth century we controlled something much better: the world's supply of oil.

On board, whaling ships represented a unique blend of egalitarianism and tyranny, and the crew—white, black, brown, Pacific Islander, Inuit—was as tatted and ethnically multiple as a Gay

Pride march in San Francisco. Herman Melville is one of America's most queer-adjacent writers, and *Moby-Dick*—book title has a hyphen, but whale's name does not—crackles with homoerotic tension. Notable pair bonds in the book include Ishmael and Queequeg, and white Ahab and black Pip. The ships themselves were durable, efficient, reliable: it took a lot of capital to send out what was basically a self-contained abattoir a year at a time, and the investors expected the whaling fleets to come back gunnels awash with spermaceti and baleen, scrimshaw and ambergris, umbrella ribs and corset stays. Whaling ships didn't really wear out; there were Nantucket boats still under canvas at the start of World War I.

*Thar she blows.* If you were alive in Los Angeles in the 1870s, whale watching would have meant going out on a Sunday to follow Palos Verdes–based crews who primarily targeted migrating gray whales, but who also had a go at humpbacks, blue whales, sei whales, and even the last of the North Pacific right whales. For many cultures, death is a spectacle, from Mayan ball courts to beheadings in Shakespeare's London to modern prize fighting. When the citizens of LA loaded a Sunday dory with hampers and parasols, one wonders whom they were rooting for—the whales or the whalers?

Many California crews were Portuguese-speaking Azorians, and they threw harpoons by hand but also used primitive grenade launchers, and if they had killed a whale, and if it didn't sink first, and if their boats hadn't been smashed to pieces in the final melee, they rowed the harvest back to shore for flensing and trying out.

A typical station was Moss Landing's. Today this harbor is a center for kayaking tours; it's a good place to see sea otters and harbor seals too. A report on whaling in California said that as of 1922, the processing facility "consisted of a large platform big enough for two or three whales at once, covered with a roof, and with an inclined plane leading up to it from the beach. Along each side of it are eighteen large wooden cooking vats heated with steam pipes. In these the various parts of the whale are placed, the flesh, skeleton, and entrails, and cooked in the process of manufacture."

The whalers' targets included sulfur-bellies, as blue whales were called then, which seems an ambitious thing to want to go after in just a rowboat (which was why they usually went out in pairs). More or less they took anything they could catch. There were no quotas, no protected species. In reviewing station records, I stopped at the inclusion of "1 bottle-nose grampus" on a random page. Risso's dolphin can be called "grampus," but I suspect the list documents not a dolphin but a Baird's beaked whale. This is a rarely seen species, even now, with mythical status; many modern mammal spotters would pay a high premium to be on the boat that finds a pod of those. I find the idea of one being killed oddly unsettling, even though it was so long ago. My reaction is not logical—death is death, either way—but reading about the kill, it feels as if somebody cleaning out a junk drawer has casually thrown away an heirloom tiara.

Society evolves, slowly but inevitably, and these days all whales are worth more alive than dead. From eating them to watching them, we have made an about-face. In this, whales have been recommodified in the same way as elk, deer, bison, bears, and beavers—food for the heart instead of food for the table. Modern whale-watching trips date from the 1950s. They started in San Diego (probably) or San Pedro (maybe), and supposedly the first tickets were a dollar each, which with inflation would be about ten dollars today. For the time, that was quite a bit of scratch. (Bowling would have been about twenty-five cents a game, and shoe rental, a dime.) Still, what a thing it was—to see a whale, in the ocean, and live to tell the story. Hard to realize there was a time when most Americans knew about whales just from the biblical story of Jonah.

That this flip happened at all is one of those hiccups in the universe that is hard now to explain. When the first whale-watching trips began, courts were just starting to desegregate schools, and the birth control pill had not yet been invented. The hero of D-Day, General Eisenhower, was US president. Where did whale-watching trips *come* from? They may have connected with a larger desire to remember the outdoors—a strong push for hunting and fishing and camping was happening then too. After World War II, as people moved from farm to city, and as city folk encountered wildlife less and less often, nature became idealized, even sentimentalized. If you are a city dweller nostalgic for authenticity and Hemingway lifestyles, going out on a boat might be an easy, one-day version of *The Old Man and the Sea.*

Now, of course, one can partake in whale and dolphin tourism all over the world, including in Sri Lanka, South Africa, New Zealand, Hawai'i, Cabo San Lucas, and the Azores. In Hong Kong you try for finless porpoise and the Indo-Pacific humpback; off of Namibia the residents are Heaviside's dolphins and Atlantic bottlenoses. Three countries—Norway, Japan, and Iceland—tie for the Janus award for hunting whales for food while also trying to develop nascent whale tourism. How can the boats' clients reconcile the discrepancy between conservation and slaughter? Perhaps the argument is to get the recalcitrant nations addicted to tourist dollars and then wean them off hunting once they perceive whales as something to see and enjoy, not as something to serve at the buffet.

Anywhere in the world, for an all-day outing, a majority of trips follow the same script. Get up in the dark, make sure you have a non-greasy breakfast (oatmeal is always safe), bring more warm clothes than Captain Scott took to Antarctica, pop a Dramamine, and queue up for the orientation and safety lecture. Boats are like analog clocks, assuming you remember those, so the front is twelve o'clock and the back is six o'clock, but the left and right—which is three and which is nine? In the excitement of the moment, even top trip leaders get them reversed.

First trip? It is good to note the location of the head (bathroom), good to put your daypack someplace dry (the cabin), and good to have brought a few five-dollar bills to tip the deckhands, who on a sportfishing trip would make money baiting hooks and filleting the catch, while on a whale-watching trip have to mop up vomit and explain which side is three o'clock over and over. Full fathom five thy father lies, so note where the lifejackets are stowed, a product you probably won't ever need, but if you do, life jackets definitely float better than Choice 2, which would be a random assemblage of picnic coolers, trash cans, small children, and empty Coke bottles.

Today we are in Monterey, going out on the *Point Sur Clipper*, fifty-five feet bow to stern and powered by two V8 diesel engines. A week ago, a half-day trip came across two Cuvier's beaked whales, which in California is even more mega rah-rah than seeing a Baird's beaked whale. Recent logbooks have detailed brown boobies and surprises like the Golden Girls, an all-matriarch orca pod. It is early November, and as krill blooms thin and calving grounds call, summer's whales slowly mosey elsewhere. By December they will be replaced by gray whales and winter birds like the wind-riding Laysan albatross, its six-foot wings as long and thin as turbine blades. In this shoulder season, it feels like we might find anything.

Leaving the dock, the cold air and the up-close sea otters help keep everybody jacked up, even those who didn't launch into the day with a double-shot espresso. Sea nettles pulse in the clear water. A belted kingfisher perches on the top of a sailboat's main mast, a black, mohawked silhouette in the orange dawn. I am ready: my longest lens and I have been waiting for such a moment. Just as I line up the shot, it flies away, its rattle call scolding in annoyance.

First stop, Coast Guard Jetty: a jumble of dark, car-sized rocks that protect the inner harbor, usually covered by a thousand aarf-aarfing California sea lions. The sandy cove just past the breakwater is San Carlos Beach; more California divers have been certified here than at any other single location, and one novice recently lost a blue snorkel, now being chewed by a puzzled sea otter. *Why does this tube worm have such a hard shell?* The captain idles the boat slowly, keeping the rocks parallel to nine o'clock. Everybody crowds the left side, photographers blazing away at the sea lions and birders checking the turnstones, hoping for a surfbird or wandering tattler. Gulls cry; crows caw; the swell splooshes against the stones. Over the faint and static-filled PA, an earnest onboard naturalist shares the requisite list of did-you-knows: sea lions can hunt for 30 hours straight, dive to 1,800 feet, swim 25 miles an hour. Secretly, I long for whimsy, even outright lies: *Did you know, the male sea lion has a penis twice the length of his body? It coils in a special organ called the schlong-korb, and on calm days, bored sea lions swim on their backs, sunning their schlong-korbs like umbrellas.*

Enough flim-flam and lollygagging. Monterey Bay Aquarium and Pacific Grove's cypress trees are on our left, and the open sea calls as the boat noses into the thickening swell and impossible egrets walk delicately on kelp mats, Jesus in white looking for crabs. I check the aquarium's smokestacks for the resident peregrine falcon but he's elsewhere today, perhaps terrorizing ducks and pigeons across the bay at Sand City. Cannery Row looks innocuous and clean from this side, even if on the ground it is all Thomas Kinkade galleries and bike rentals and gourmet fudge depots. I remember the days pre-resurrection, when Cannery Row was still wooden, raw, and derelict: Steinbeck's character Doc, based on the real-life biologist Ed Ricketts, wouldn't have liked this new Monterey at all. Ricketts died in Monterey in 1948, killed by a train while crossing Drake Avenue, and once told John Steinbeck that children must be very wise and patient to tolerate adults at all.

As we head out, an outflow of seabirds paces us. Undulating lines of surf scoters, skeins of pelagic cormorants, hundreds of penguin-colored common murres—all the morning birds are heading seaward, agreeing with our choice of direction, even if motivated by different hungers.

"Oh, shit—" None of us is ready when the first whale of the day shows up, a probable humpback half a mile out past one o'clock. We chase it but never catch up. In the future I suppose all the tour boats will get instant updates from a fleet of Google-sponsored drones, or will be able to sweep side to side using sonar so sensitive it can locate a dropped tin of Skoal in two hundred fathoms of water, but for now we all search for whales the old-fashioned way, the Ahab and the *Pequod* way, the way that humans have done since the time of cave art and walrus-skin umiaks. We have just our eyes, our attention, our ability to isolate the one from the many. I have brought $3,000 German binoculars and a messenger bag filled with bird books and cetacean guides, but it all begins with the act of looking. On this trip we share the duties equally, trying to stay alert. Passengers and crew adjust Ray-Bans and drift into daydream and snap back to the present, and most look down-sun, not up-sun, trying to tell if over there, *there*, if that splashy little whitecap is just the chop sorting itself out or if it is the final twirl of a dissipating spout.

In theory one can ID whales to species using the height and

shape of their blows, but most spouts only hang in place half a minute before dissolving into mist and longing. I try not to get distracted by the too-distant gulls, by the bobbing white floats marking prawn pots on the bottom, by the urgent question of whether or not it's too early in the day to eat my first sandwich. Tricky thing, the ocean, a deceit-show of shift and blurs. Nothing is ever as it seems. Fronds of kelp wave like sea turtle flippers; plastic bags look like jellies and jellies look like plastic bags; a gang of porpoising sea lions breaks the surface with the same sleek, torpedoing motion as a pod of the larger, much rarer northern right whale dolphin. "What's that—oh, never mind." Everybody wants to help spot; nobody wants to be the first duffer to raise a false alarm.

What color is the ocean? Snot green, says James Joyce, yet it is equally true to admit that when the sun opens a slit in the clouds like a solid silver letter opener, the water shines brighter than abalone. The amount of open water that wind travels across is called fetch; fetch plus windspeed allows one to guestimate swell, which generally builds over long distances. Rogue waves defy simple averages, and buoys verify that there can be seventy-five-footers in the right (wrong?) conditions. Names for the sea, if you are an Anglo-Saxon poet: seal bath, fish home, whale road. My names? Pearl hoarder, swell pusher, sky mirror, joy giver.

The fishing boats and other whale-watching trips all share

locations and sightings by radio. Plenty of whales to go around; the boats practice one-for-all, all-for-one. "Orca, orca," gets every boat revved up and headed that way, ours included. We are heading north-northeast at ten knots, aiming the boat to cross over a subsurface feature at right angles. The whales understand what we can't hear, see, or taste, which is how the ocean roars with life, with energy, with the comings and goings of currents and eddies and downdrafts and thermoclines and the vertical lift and fall of a trillion bundles of supercharged DNA. Underneath the boat there are superhighways of water rising and falling, crossing and rearranging, and underneath us too is an alpine geology of seamounts and side canyons, badlands and thrust faults, all of it feeding down into the dark mysteries of the actual Monterey Bay main canyon.

Cold water flows downslope off the edges of this grander-than-Grand-Canyon-canyon; abyssal water rises to fill the void, bringing a rich soup of nutrients closer to the surface where the sunlight is. Over five hundred species of fish live here, plus the thousands of non-fish things like crabs and jellies and nudi-branchs and sea stars and *Octopus rubescens,* the East Pacific red octopus, also known as the ruby octopus, allegedly very good at getting out of its tank in laboratories. Small to large, everything interconnects: plant plankton and krill feed whale and whale lice alike. Bow *namaste* when meeting the great chain of being.

You can rely on birds to be good journalists when it comes to reporting on water status and food sources. At sea, whenever the bird action picks up, experienced whale watchers know to be ready for something good. I can tell we've reached the edge of the canyon because after a fairly blank crossing, now the shearwaters begin wheeling past the front of the boat. Smaller than gulls, they peel and bank, rise and dip, using the lift of wind shear off the surface of waves to arc to the next wave and the next. In between, their knife-blade wings beat in rapid bursts—fly, glide, fly, glide, soar up high, rollercoaster down low; skim the wave face so close that wingtips cut the surface, trailing razor slits of black bubbles.

Upwelling has been working overtime here, and rafts of full-bellied sooty shearwaters bob in the water like drowsy ducks, staying put until the boat crosses some invisible DMZ and they decide to try to get airborne, feet pedaling on the surface and wings bashing up and down like cartoon gooney birds too fat to fly. Sometimes they make it and sometimes they just give up and settle back in the water with a *plop*, looking cross that we have interrupted their postprandial contemplations.

Look! *There there there there—*

Ah, terrific, we finally have whales, and lots of them. Bushy, columnar blow; stocky, midsized body; knuckle-ridged back ending in a hump-mounted fin...probably a humpback; when it upends the large white tail flukes and punches into a vertical dive, that cinches it. I am interested in more than just general species ID. If I can get a clear shot of the tail from behind as a humpback dives, the pattern of scars and barnacles serves as a cetacean fingerprint. As marine mammals go, humpbacks show a lot of personality, not just in their actions (lunge feeding, lobtailing, flipper slapping) but also in their pinto pony splotchiness. Each tail is unique, as are the front flippers. There's a master photo data set of tails and flippers, and if you upload your images to the Happywhale website, they'll email you back a name (if the humpback has one), plus updates if others spot your find weeks or even years later.

The closest whale is back up now, and in zooming in on my shots, I see that on the trailing edge of its tail are clusters of acorn barnacles, and on top of those, something that looks like a string of pink snot, trailing behind as if the whale has stepped in gum. That is the rabbit-ear barnacle, one of a half dozen crustacean species that give up on life in the tidepools and set out to see the world courtesy of a host whale. Smart choice, since the whale moves forward constantly, allowing a rush of food-rich water to flow past the barnacle's ready filters. No downtime, either. Unless the whale strands itself or is intersected by a harpoon, for the barnacle it is perpetually high tide, all day, every day.

Knocking off barnacles may be one reason humpbacks shoot up tall and crash down hard. The barnacle is not a parasite (it does not feed directly on the whale's body), but the collective weight and friction of the barnacles creates significant drag, and for the same reason that Navy ships need to be drydocked, sandblasted clean, and recoated with a new layer of antifouling paint, so too do some whales need to reduce the amount of scabby, crusty protrusions they are schlepping along day and night, up-ocean and down. Erupting out of the water and smashing back down could be a way to do this.

Or then again, maybe that's not the main reason.

Maybe it just feels good.

Maybe it is a way to show off to the other whales. "Yeehaw, look at *me*."

Maybe it is a simple Morse code message—two big splashes and a tail wag tells the other whales, "Hey guys, wait up."

Maybe it is something sexual, boa-flirty and erotic.

Maybe it is a warning: look, you pesky shark you, back off or I will squash you like a bug.

Blue whales breech too, and gray whales spyhop, but to get the full whale show, one needs to find a group of in-the-mood humpbacks. In California in summer, that is usually not hard. Once on a trip from Half Moon Bay to the Farallon Islands and back, I kept track of every single whale I could see. It was a calm day, and by sundown I had counted six blue whales, two fin whales, two thousand Risso's dolphins, and eighty-eight different humpbacks. (To count dolphins, superimpose an imaginary circle on the water, count what's inside that circle, then count how many circles there are until you run out of dolphins—or run out of water. Keep a running track on index cards or in your pocket notebook. You brought a notebook, didn't you? Of course you did.)

I am looking left when there's a commotion on the other side. We've had a really close encounter and people are laughing and wiping their faces. "Wow, did you see that?" Tour boats are not supposed to crowd the whales, but whales come and go based on their own needs, not any concern about regulations. Sometimes one launches up so close everybody gets soaked by the splash when it comes back down. That's exciting and yet unnerving, since you suddenly realize the boat is only upright and not smashed in two because the whale has decided to leave it alone. Humans are above all the other animals until we are not.

Writers can't agree about how to narrate this exuberance. "A breaching whale is a ladder to the bottom of the sea"—Gregory Colbert—while Robert Lowell, memorializing his dead cousin, describes a rising and falling whale as "upward angel, downward fish." I prefer the perspective of UK naturalist Mark Carwardine, somebody who has had the pleasure of many thousands of humpback sightings. In an otherwise sober and technical overview of the species, he ends up using words like spectacular, inquisitive, rowdy, playful.

Is that okay? Can we talk about nature in the same way that we talk about our children, our neighbors, our Lucy dogs from the pound?

Sure, why not. We can be dour tomorrow. Today just be human, and in our humanity, take pleasure in the pleasure of other sentient beings around us. Pure neutrality is overrated (besides being impossible to achieve).

I didn't know it yet, but a surprise act was about to crash the set. Whale-watching is like a Bruce Springsteen concert—which unexpected guest star will show up to crush the encore? In this case, it was the biggest of the big guys. First it was a blue whale, then another, and then in a rare congruence of red-hot luck, fin whales as well. At one point, in the same view, I had two blue whales (largest animal on earth), one fin whale (second largest), and two humpback whales. This was all from the same railing on the boat, looking out at the same piece of ocean. I couldn't even take a picture, I was so gobsmacked.

Just under the surface, blue whales look not just blue but electric turquoise. Fin whales are nearly as long, but they look fifty shades of sleek gray, and that is one way to tell the two species apart. The blue whale also has a small fin (small in relation to the whale itself) shoved way back down the back near the tail, almost like an afterthought, while a fin whale's dorsal fin is larger and closer to midships. *Sppiffff*—you can hear the blow from a fair distance off. As a plume of warm, wet breath condensing in the cool air, a blue whale's blow can geyser thirty-five feet, and, if the light catches it just so, it shines rainbow iridescent. (If the boat motors through it, it smells fishy.)

They didn't always used to be like this, so capacious and enspeciated. In the fossil past, baleen whales were small—many of them hardly bigger than a VW bus. That works fine if food is relatively evenly distributed. Shifts in winds and currents four million years ago made it advantageous to be large: prey concentrations changed, and it was better when plowing through a dense cloud of krill if you could hoover up a lot of food at once. It was better too if you had the reserves to help you get from food source to food source, even if the search took months. Small was out; big was in.

There are more species of big whales known today than when I was a kid, though blue whales are still the boss. If we arrange the rorqual clan largest to smallest like the von Trapp children in *Sound of Music*, then the list currently goes like this: blue, fin, sei, Bryde's, Eden's, Omura's, regular Minke, Antarctica Minke, and possibly an as-yet-unnamed species, the dwarf Minke. Newest of all, the Rice's whale lives in the Gulf of Mexico; it formerly was thought of as a subpopulation of Bryde's whale, until closer study proved otherwise. Some of these you may not have heard of, and it takes a bit of globe-trotting to see them all in the wild—I have not finished yet, but I am getting closer, one trip at a time. (If I had to pick between Ahab and Ishmael, my checklists tell me who I most resemble. And yes, I read the book and saw the movie: if I am indeed Ahab, we all know what happens in the end.)

Even if I am motivated by unclean desires—my horrid life list and all of that—the resulting experiences are still worth the price of admission. This trip today has already been brilliant, and just when I think the day can't get any better, the captain lines us up parallel to a swimming blue whale and switches off the engines, letting momentum carry us forward. Silence and whale breath and silence and the slap of water against hull and silence and whale and there is hardly any barrier between us at all—no throbbing engines, no exhaust fumes, no attempt to turn the boat left or right to keep up. Just water and whales and I am happy, truly and deeply happy.

It's hard to be happy in the world. Nature is one way to fill the ballast tanks back up. Not the only way of course, but one way, one very reliable way.

Some theories of aesthetics say full pleasure has to come from dark and light mixed together. Shakespeare knows when to have a moment of comedy or wordplay lighten the mood, before going back to eating babies and maiming eyes. So should the boat catch fire now, or a squid's giant tentacle slither over the railing and drag away one of the minor characters?

I vote no.

The darkness is out there, but let's hold off on experiencing it, thinking about it, admitting that we are all just sinners in the hands of an angry god, at least until we get back to the dock.

Besides all the whales, this has been a good birdy day. Cassin's auklets are stubby maritime puffinlets, robin-small and dark gray. You only see them from boats like this, and today so far my index cards tell me I have seen thirty-two. They nest in burrows on sea cliffs and offshore islands, and only come in to those at night. To see them at all, you need to be out with the pelagic birders and the whale watchers. Looking at one closely through my very expensive binoculars I realize how much they remind me of deflated footballs, with a flick of white curling above each eye like a surprised apostrophe.

Hours have passed, and among other things, I need to transfer my pocket tallies into my main journal. I review what I've written in it so far, which includes the essential fact that "If you tape a magnet to an elephant seal's forehead, it gets lost." A biologist from Cal State Humboldt said that, so it must be true. (The seal gets lost, not the magnet.) Somebody asks me if I have seen the elephant seal species that lives in Antarctica (yes). What about a narwhal? No, I am saving that to be mammal number 1,000. I did once almost buy a medieval narwhal tusk from a dealer in Paris. We then share narwhal trivia, including double-tusked males and the footnote that 15 percent of female narwhals grow tusks too.

A lull in sightings allows me a chance to turn and survey a full circle of horizon. It blurs and shakes, since I am tired and it's time to clean my lenses, but inside the Zeiss glass is a world of infinite texture and crenellation. Water is never static, never plain; it heaves and rolls; it shimmies, jostles, allegros, and collapses; it teases the horizon, promising distance yet never revealing a clean edge. Up close, there is a nervous chaos that excites us but excludes us: the scale of motion is planetary, not human. And the answer to the question, *What color is the sea?* is another question shot right back: *What color* isn't *it?* In the boat's shadow, the passing water reflects our white hull; flecks of carmine are seaweed tassels torn loose in a storm; the Sabine's gull's bill tip is a spike of pure yellow glowing at the end of saturated black. Earlier in the week a boat reported finding a basking shark on the surface, its skin dappled yellow as a newborn fawn. The ocean holds more colors than we have words for, and the English language is like an eager dog on the beach that rushes up to the surf line then falls back, overwhelmed by the enormity of all that water.

Ours is one of the all-day trips, and after hours of looking, people are growing weary. Eyes burn with smeared sunscreen; salt spray rimes every lens; some of the passengers are queasy from the times we stopped to wait for whales and were rocked hard by cross-swell. Nobody has thrown up yet, but for some people, *mal de mer* clearly waits close at hand—perhaps just one more lurch away. You can see it in their faces and their slumped, defeated postures.

So I have just seen a whale, probably another humpback, and nobody else has noticed. People doze, or try convince themselves they do not look green, or fossick for lost gloves in the bottom of infinite daypacks. Should I say something? Of course—after all, this is a whale trip, and people paid good money to be here. On the other hand, the beast in question is far away and might be gone before we even get halfway there. I search the horizon in one more slow circle: ocean, ocean, ocean, whale, ocean, ocean. The animal is a small piece of a large landscape. It does not need us, and, ultimately, we do not need it, not right now, not today. I let it go. John Keats, *Endymion:* "The gulfing whale was like a dot in the spell."

Sore knees and a slanting sun tell us all that the afternoon has worn on. It's later than many of us realize, and we're not back yet. "Let's turn this pig down-swell," I hear the captain say to the mate. He means that it's time to aim for port, and to do so on a vector that has the swell coming from directly behind us, which will add speed and lessen the barf factor.

Secretly, I am glad we're heading back. I pretend to be the flinty heart of the hard core (to quote Christopher Leahy), but in actuality I have a bum leg, and by now it aches like cold iron, plus

I've eaten all the healthy food in my bag and have started to graze the snack table in the main cabin. Oreos remind me of childhood, and I twist them open to scrape out the white lard with my teeth. *Stop that right now. What if your doctor saw that?* I've also taken too many pictures—my high-capacity memory cards are nowhere near full, but some poor schmuck, namely me, will have to sort out these 952 images later. Most show water only, the place where the whale just *was*, though there is a substantial mix of blurry seagulls and the ass-ends of shearwaters. File, *delete*; file, *delete*—I can already predict how my dinner hour will be spent.

Ask people to draw a whale and they usually sketch a sperm whale, boxy headed and crowned with a fire hydrant spout, the spume flourishing majestically, like a bouquet in a vase. This animal goes deep, deep, deep to hunt giant squid, diving into the blackest, deepest levels of the ocean. I find myself thinking about darkness, the cold, the immense pressures, the green flickers of bioluminescent fish: what a strange and primordial world that must be. Sperm whale dives can last ninety minutes and go below 3,000 feet. (Light rarely penetrates past the first 600 feet.) Even more record-worthy, a Cuvier's beaked whale has been documented at a depth of 9,816 feet. That is 9,000 feet deeper than Navy submarines operate at, just for comparison. Come on humans, show some ambition.

Nearly all whales will go that deep eventually. At first, a dead whale floats, bloated and putrid, providing food for the sharks below and the gulls above. After a few days or a few weeks, the carcass will sink—sink or wash ashore—and if it sinks, that creates what is called "whale fall." Some studies claim that in any given five-year span, our ocean floors may be enhanced by as many as half a million dead whales.

I am strangely attracted to deep water yet repulsed at the same time. The fact is, I can paddle a kayak but I cannot swim a lick, and even just snorkeling, I wear a life jacket strapped rib-crushing tight and I kick my fins furiously, hard up against the ragged edge of terror. In Baja or the Maldives I am voraciously eager to see it all, touch it all, know it all, and yet at the same time, my primordial lizard brain is screaming *abort, abort,* as it tries to get me to turn around and thrash my way back to the safety and normalcy of shallow water.

Earlier we had come across a pod of curious Pacific white-sided dolphins, attracted to the boat's pressure wave and flashing along each side to have a turn at bow-riding. They came from stern to front, sprinting to match our speed and then surfing tight against the vee of the bow wave. Ride over, they would peel off, drop back, then circle around to go again. As I leaned over the railing for photographs, I had a vivid image of swaying a few inches too far and going in headfirst. With complete certainty I knew what would happen next: I knew I would go straight down like a two-ton stone. I dreaded it and yet expected it, nearly longed for it. Going down, I would be thinking, "The worst thing has finally happened, *just as I always knew it would.*"

There's a scene halfway through *Moby-Dick* when the Pequod's crew kills an old, crippled whale, and in trying to dismember it, they discover the whale has a stone-tipped harpoon from a previous hunt buried deep inside its body. The weapon is ancient, perhaps even antediluvian. They feel wonder and horror at encountering an animal so unnaturally old. The passage implies that it was not unusual to find an assortment of weapons buried in recently killed whales; a hand-thrown lance was not always lethal, and some whales got away. What was exceptional was the antiquity of the harpoon, not its presence buried in living flesh.

How often we make nature bear the weight of our casual murders and shifting appetites. Melville was writing a work of deep fiction, as prophetic and prescient as any American novel from the nineteenth century, but in echoing his narrative, recent discoveries confirm his dark vision. In 2007 Inupiat hunters killed a bowhead whale, and in harvesting the carcass, they found a harpoon point from the 1880s buried in its shoulder. That made the whale at least 130 years old. In 1992, an even earlier artifact was found; deep inside the body of a modern whale was an indigenous spearhead of a style last crafted in the mid-nineteenth century.

Prompted by those morbid revelations, cetacean researchers came up with a way to age bowhead whales by measuring the lens of the eye, and if the methodology is correct, they have found whales who are 135, 172, and even 211 years old. Are all the whales out there in their hundreds? If the data are correct, each of these measured animals lived through the worst of the whaling eras, historic and modern. What wounds and memories they must carry inside their bodies, their hearts, their troubled, chthonic souls. I confess I identify with such relicts, and probably too much so. I feel like we're not-so-distant cousins. I don't just mean my actual scars—cancer and stitched cuts and broken hands and the $70,000 in surgical titanium holding my right leg together—but all of it, inside and out, including the sad parts of my childhood and the thousand times I know now I could have been a better parent, a more patient teacher, a more astute spouse.

Even so, we go on, each of us. Sitting in the late slant sun on the back of a boat, salt lipped, slit eyed, gull lifted, I finally can hear what the water has been trying to tell me all day, and that is that none of us should be in mourning, or at least not for long, but instead should use the last of the light to write a thank-you note to the gods. There are indeed such animals as whales (we did not kill them all)—*thank you.* And that there is a color the Romans knew, *glaucous,* and it is not blue, not gray, not green, but all of those at once, and while we may no longer have a word for that hue, it is out there, and water can be that color, and today I saw it, so *thank you*. We crossed a wall of baitfish, and birds circled the boat like ecstatic confetti, and I don't even know what kind they were, but *thank you*. Good friends wait for me on land, and the simple pleasures of hot baths and warm beds. *Thank you.* Somewhere inside the cloud chamber that is my camera waits a perfect picture of a dolphin. If I wake up tonight and stand at the hotel window, no matter how late it is, I will hear the distant sea lions talking each to each. If I listen just a bit longer, I might hear a great horned owl. I do believe I deserve to be happy, but it still stuns me to be *this* happy. If I want to go back out tomorrow, and the day after tomorrow, and even the day after that, there will be a boat ready to do that, and if not a boat, then a kayak or just a piece of the shore where I can sit and look and write and think. If the blue whales migrate away, then the gray whales will fill in their places, and when they finally get done with California and go off to Alaska, something else will be here instead, maybe an orca, maybe a beaked whale, maybe the first right whale in a hundred years, or maybe some new and marvelous creature never spoken of before in the history of science. I am sorry if I am blinking like such a newbie. I never thought I would get this far, to be honest, to be allowed to see and feel so much. Whatever holy stick magicked this day into existence, and whatever

rod drove us forward and herded the clouds in the sky and beat
out such an exact and perfect tempo—

*Thank you.*

Photo by Amber Hood

# About the Author

Poet and essayist **Charles Hood** grew up next to the Los Angeles River and has been a factory worker, ski instructor, boat salesman, and birding guide. He stopped counting birds when his list reached 5,000, but he soon replaced it with a mammal list, which now nears 1,000. His awards include a Fulbright Scholarship; Artist-in-Residencies with the National Science Foundation, the Center for Land Use Interpretation, and the Annenberg Beach House; a Research Fellowship with the Center of Art + Environment at the Nevada Museum of Art; and a Playa art and science residency. *Wild LA*, his book sponsored by the Natural History Museum of Los Angeles County, was named a Best Nonfiction Book of 2019. Charles has birded all fifty states, plus jungles and deserts from Tibet to Patagonia and New Guinea to Mongolia. Along the way, he has shared seal meat with an Inuit family, eaten fried mopani worms in Zambia, kayaked in the South Pacific, and mountain biked in Antarctica. He currently lives and teaches in the Antelope Valley, and is the author of Heyday's *A Californian's Guide to the Birds Among Us*, as well as forthcoming books on reptiles, nature after dark, and the California wine country.

# Acknowledgments

Some ideas for "Audubon's Tiny Houses" appeared in the second-ever issue of *Catamaran Literary Reader*, buried inside an essay about condors; many years later, an expanded version of the Audubon piece appeared in their thirtieth issue. "Cochineal and the Color Red" first appeared in *Catamaran,* and the initial premise of "I Heart Ugly Nature" made itself known in a *Catamaran* essay titled "In Praise of Ugly Nature." "Landscape with Unicorns and Barnacles" was recently in *Catamaran* as well. The title "Confessions of an Amateur" quotes an essay by Bill Vaughn in *Crunge VII.* A section of "Lure of the List" was published as *"Le Docteur* in Morocco," *Santa Monica Review.* An early version of "Two Thousand Palm Trees" first appeared as "The Perfect Theology of Palm Trees," *Western Humanities Review.* Bobcat photo (page 106) courtesy of John Haubrich. "Booby Gannet" (page 168) courtesy of the John James Audubon Center at Mill Grove,

Montgomery County Audubon Collection, and Zebra Publishing. Friends, librarians, reviewers, pathfinders, and companions: gratitude and humble reverence to David Abel, Jeffrey Ahmad, Chas Anderson, Karen Baker, Mark Beaman, Jean Michel Bompar, John Bruce, Paul Carter, Carol Chambers, Matt Coolidge, Sally Crosby, Sam Deges, Kelly Fernandez, William Fox, Joan Fry, Kristin Friedrich, the merry elves at Grassy Knoll Industries, Michael Guista, Jon Hall, Abbey Hood, Amber Hood, Matthew Jaffe, Cole Justice, Shannon Knab, Michael Light, Roger Linfield, Doug Manuel, José Gabriel Martínez-Fonseca, Elizabeth McKenzie, David Mehler, Vivek Menon, Kathryn Mitchell, Larry Mitchell, the captains, deckhands, and naturalists with Monterey Bay Whale Watch, Christine Mugnolo, Zia Nisani, Robert Peters, Playa Arts Foundation, Carolyn Purnell, Mike Richardson, Venkat Sankar, Catherine Segurson, Kate Spencer, Sharon Taylor, Phil Telfer, William Vaughn, Erin Westeen, John Wright, Callyn Yorke.

And to my friends at Heyday, thank you for making books even in times of plague and doubt: Emmerich Anklam, Julie Coryell, Emily Grossman, Ashley Ingram, Diane Lee, Malcolm Margolin, Christopher Miya, Marthine Satris, Steve Wasserman, Gayle Wattawa, and Molly Woodward. To quote Jenny Offill, I owe each and every one of you a pony.